GREED
TO
GREEN

GREED
TO
GREEN

The transformation of an industry and a life

David Gottfried

Foreword by Paul Hawken

WorldBuild Publishing

WorldBuild Publishing
A division of WorldBuild Technologies Inc.
2342 Shattuck Avenue, #411
Berkeley, CA 94704
www.worldbuild.com

Author's Note: Some of the names and locations mentioned in the book have been changed to protect the parties.

Illustrations by James Thurber, from his book *The Last Flower*, ©1939. Reprinted here by arrangement with Rosemary A. Thurber and The Barbara Hogenson Agency. All rights reserved.

ISBN 0-9744326-0-1
Library of Congress Control Number: 2003097486

WorldBuild is committed to helping build a sustainable world. This book is printed with soy inks on acid-free New Leaf EcoBook 100 paper that is 100% postconsumer waste content and has been processed chlorinefree. This printing saved 45 trees, 2,000 pounds of solid waste, 19,000 gallons of water, 28 million BTUs of energy, and 4,200 pounds of greenhouse gases.

Design and Production: Seventeenth Street Studios
Copy editor: Anne Canright
Printed and bound in Canada by Friesens

To my parents Ira and Judith:
For their unceasing love and teachings

To green pioneers and councils all over the world

CONTENTS

Foreword	ix
Acknowledgments	xiii
The Earth Commandments	xv

Part One: Greed

1. A Vision of Green	3
2. Florsheims to Ferragamos	11
3. The Go-Go '80s	17
4. Her Dress Was the Color of Money	37
5. The Seeds of Green	53

Part Two: Green

6. Down and Out in San Francisco	79
7. Starting the Council	93
8. Phone Calls, Faxes, and Frappuccinos	103
9. Building the Organization	119
10. On My Own Again	139
11. My Dinner with Rick	163
12. A Zealot? Me?	179
13. Show Me the (Internet) Money!	193
14. GBC Goes Global	205
15. Austin 2002	219
16. Greening My Life	233

FOREWORD

MARTHA GRAHAM, THE GREAT DANCER and choreographer, once described the creative process as "blessed unrest." The same could be said of David Gottfried. Despite his good fortune in the conventional world of real estate development, he was blessed with unrest, his unceasing curiosity and concern. Anyone who knows or has met David can feel the energy. It is a toe-tapping, eye-flashing kinetic that takes on any challenge. What he took on was the building and construction industry and its relationship to living systems. He took on the biggest industry in the world. As I said, blessed unrest.

Sustainability is about the relationship between the two most complex systems on earth—human and living systems. The interrelationship between these two systems marks every person's existence and underlines the rise and fall of every civilization. While the word sustainability is relatively new, every culture has confronted this relationship for better or ill. Historically, no civilization has reversed its tracks with respect to the environment but rather has declined and disappeared because it forfeited its own habitat. For the first time in history, a civilization—its people, companies, and governments—are trying to arrest this slide and understand how to live on earth. This is a watershed in human existence.

To say this book is about the power of one person to change the world, though true, would be a cliché. This book is not about David, sustainability, or even green buildings. It is about the mystery of change. Although it is axiomatic that everything changes, it is a mystery as to *how* things change. What we have here is a first-person and animated account of how things have and did change. When you read it, you will draw your own conclusions. It is about pluck and determination. And it is about timing, hard work, and manufactured luck. But it is about conviction above all. Not the conviction that makes others wrong, but the affirmation of what is right and what is possible. I have heard David speak several times in my life, and without doubt, what he shares above all is enthusiasm, a word that comes from the Greek roots *en theos* meaning "within God." I have said that if this movement toward a green and just world is to succeed, it will be because we will build a more interesting sandbox for everyone to play in. That is what David did: He founded and helped build the most important green trade organization in the world. There is virtually no second place. Thousands of people and companies are playing inside it, creating the best standards in the world. Nothing compares with the growth, magnitude, and import of the U.S. Green Building Council. No one has done the metrics, but I believe it is safe to say that no organization has had a bigger impact on the environment than this one in terms of energy and materials saved, toxins eliminated, greenhouse gases avoided, and human health enhanced. And it is just the beginning.

It could be said that every person has the responsibility to live in their time. This is our time: stunning in its promise, terrifying in its direction. David is living now. In *Greed to Green* he shares this passage. He is brilliant, yes. But he is also Everyman. He has weaknesses and longings and aversions just as we all do. In sharing himself and the fabric of a life well directed, we can find ourselves and know that little or nothing exceeds our grasp if we love the world as well as David has.

—Paul Hawken
Sausalito, California

ACKNOWLEDGMENTS

WITHOUT THE INCREDIBLE coaching of Adair Lara, my development editor, I'd still be working on unpublished versions of this book. Her vision, strength of character, quick wit, and ability to get the most out of me made the book a reality.

Special thanks and deep appreciation to Mischa Schwartzmann for years of urging me to sit down and write this story.

To Sara, my love, for changing my life. To my cousins in D.C. for their love, teachings, and generosity, and my brothers Glenn and Richard for their love and constant support.

There are so many others to sincerely thank: Rick Fedrizzi and Mike Italiano for their continuing friendship and encouragement in building the council, Christine Ervin and Pegi Shriver for their support and leadership, Kristin Ralff Douglas for keeping the USGBC flame alive, Jeff Davis for his unrelenting friendship, the late David Brower for his vision, Gil Masters for his inspiration, Chuck Angyal for his friendship and help launching my consulting career, Che Wall for his leadership in Australia and with the World Green Building Council, Dorothy Divack and Kenneth Ullman for help creating a green life, and to all of the members and staff of the U.S. and World Green Building councils who have helped us change the world.

THE EARTH COMMANDMENTS

MY GOOD FRIEND AND MENTOR, David Brower, died in November 2000. David was eighty-eight and had lived a full life. His lifework, strength of vision, and personality inspired us to work for a better Earth: one based on conservation, preservation, and restoration—"CPR." In his years he scaled hundreds of mountains, making seventy first ascents; he was the first executive director of the Sierra Club; and he founded Friends of the Earth, the League of Conservation Voters, and Earth Island Institute. He also helped create numerous national parks: Point Reyes, Cape Cod, and Fire Island National Seashores; Kings Canyon, North Cascades, Redwood, and Great Basin National Parks—all benefited from his passionate attachment to the American land. He was nominated for the Nobel Peace Prize three times.

Several years before he died, David challenged me to undertake a short writing project. The world, he said, had changed so much since Moses came down from Mt. Sinai with the Ten Commandments that we now needed to amend those directives, by including guidelines for our relationship with Earth.

I recruited my good friend and teacher Mischa Schwartzmann, a retired English professor, writer, and photographer, to help me take a modest shot at this task. When we presented the five Earth Commandments to David Brower at Sinbad's, his favorite restaurant along the San Francisco Bay waterfront, David came up with the sixth one.

1. We shall live in harmony with all life that flies through the air, swims in the waters, walks on the land, and that which remains rooted.

2. We shall protect and preserve the Earth and all living systems for all generations.

3. We shall restore that which has been damaged, especially the air, water, and soil.

4. We shall not multiply beyond the capacity of Earth to sustain itself and all of life.

5. We shall embrace and cherish the Planet Earth, as we were born to it; and together we shall become stewards of its future.

6. What have we forgotten?

Part One: Greed

CHAPTER 1

A Vision of Green

"IN NATURE THERE IS NO WASTE." Bill McDonough's voice boomed out to the audience of thousands in Boston's convention center. He wore a yellow bow tie and gray suit, and his long hair rested on his shoulders. I scribbled notes in shorthand, sitting forward in my seat in an effort to capture every word, stopping now and then to shake the cramp out of my hand. McDonough said forcefully from the podium, "We must design our buildings so that they mimic natural systems." The conference had a green theme, focusing on sustainability: the preservation and conservation of resources for future generations as these apply to buildings.

It was 1992, and I was in Boston for the annual American Institute of Architects national convention—at which the International Union of Architects' World Congress was also meeting. All around me I heard foreign languages: Chinese, Spanish, German.

Among all those architects, I felt a bit like a duck out of water. I couldn't even tell you what I was doing there. I was a real estate developer—one of the enemy. We carted buildings off to the dump and replaced them with new ones, sometimes even the same size and shape, as we had done at our firm.

I was thirty-two and had worked for my cousins, Diane and Jim Katz, in Washington, D.C., since graduating from Stanford *1982* ten years before. The real estate market was dismal in the early '90s, and Diane and Jim wanted to diversify. I'd read a *Time* magazine feature article on the business opportunities in greening the environment and so, a few months later, found myself at this convention.

Since arriving two days before, I had been unable to sleep. My mind raced. I hadn't heard such impassioned discussion about the future of our planet since I was a sophomore taking a civil engineering solar energy class at Stanford. "We Americans like to waste," Professor Gil Masters had said at our first class meeting in 1980. "We consume about 20 percent of the world's energy, even though we comprise 5 percent of the population." I hadn't given a thought to the physical state of the earth and how our consumption affects it since I was a boy in L.A. during the 1970s water and energy crises. At the time, my dad wouldn't let us water the lawn, flush a pee, or take long showers. A few years later the utility rates had shot up because of power shortages, and he'd yell at us if we left the lights on. Shortly thereafter, during the oil embargo we'd wait in line for as much as an hour at the gas station.

In Professor Masters's class, students could design and make a scale-model solar home of balsa wood instead of taking the final. I spent hours on my model, giving it a solar-heated Jacuzzi, an insulating rooftop garden, and an indoor basketball court heated by a passive solar water wall. I was so pleased with how the model came out that it gained a permanent place of honor on a living room shelf, going with me every time I moved.

When I began my career as a developer, though, I lost track of my idealism; sporadic attempts to implement innovative designs

sputtered out. "What about installing solar hot water in the apartments?" I asked Diane at one of our management meetings.
"That's cute," she said. "But this isn't California. People don't
go for that stuff out here." I shrugged, as if to say, "Yeah, right,
dumb idea."

An architect named Randy Croxton was at the podium now.
"Here's a 100,000-square-foot green historic renovation I'm doing
for the National Audubon Society building in New York," he said,
pointing at a photograph of the ornate 1891 George Post building
projected on a large screen. "We're designing new energy-efficient
mechanical and electrical systems for this nine-story full renovation and penthouse addition. We'll use 70 percent less energy than
a conventional code-compliant office building." I scribbled what
he said on my pad. My pen ran out of ink midway, and I searched
my pockets for another one.

In the next slide a graph showed the green building elements
Croxton planned to use: healthy paints and glues, efficient lights
with occupancy sensors and daylight dimmers, four recycling
chutes running the full height of the building, water-efficient urinals and faucets, and all natural, undyed carpet made from 100
percent natural wool. They'd also installed a superefficient gas-
fired absorption heater-chiller. In our developments in D.C., we
met the building code requirements for water and energy efficiency and not a bit more. We picked building materials according to price and market trends, never giving a thought to where
they came from or where they would end up. No one did, in
those days.

The conference lunch was served in an enormous adjoining
room. There were a hundred tables, each seating ten or twelve
people. I didn't know anyone, so I picked a table at random. We

all introduced ourselves. A few of my tablemates were from Mexico; another was from Hong Kong, and the rest were from the United States. All of them were architects. As we were getting acquainted, the lunch facilitator's voice boomed from a loudspeaker: "Now, I want each table to work together as a team. For the next thirty minutes, your mission is to design the world of the year 2020. How can we make it sustainable?" Each group would get thirty seconds to present its ideas to the room.

On my pad, I wrote down the key categories that came to mind: energy, water, waste, transportation, community, products, education, and work. The others at the table did the same. We then appointed one of our number to serve as a scribe for our flipchart. About forty and from Vermont, he wore a black turtleneck, khaki pants, and a huge smile.

"How about energy?" our scribe asked, when he'd taken his place by the oversized paper pad, felt-tip pen in hand. "What power sources and types of systems do we envision in 2020? What will our buildings and transportation systems look like?" He sketched the outline of several buildings and graphed the direction of the sun—east to west. Then he drew solar collectors, a large fuel cell, and several gas-fired microturbines.

"All power will come from the sun, from solar and hydrogen based systems," a man from Mexico offered, looking at notes he'd written with an antique fountain pen. He spoke excellent English, with a strong Spanish accent. His notes looked like pieces of art, with small sketches across the top and perfectly formed letters below.

"We need to redesign our communities," a woman from Boston chimed in. She looked at us fiercely. "I walk to local stores to buy all my groceries. I also work at home and don't own a car, but there aren't a lot of people who are willing or able to live the way I do." As I listened, I realized with some embarrassment what little thought I gave to driving all over the place. I thought of Third Street in Santa Monica, close to where I grew up, which had recently been closed to traffic. As a result it had become a place for people to dine, but also to stroll, sit on a bench, or visit with neighbors by a fountain. Soon street performers appeared and then new stores, as a higher-end pedestrian-oriented niche market began to flourish. Santa Monica had taken a busy, smog-creating thoroughfare and turned it into a prosperous, environmentally friendly promenade.

As I thought about that, a tingle ran through me—not quite an idea, but a relative of one. "We're getting too far from community," I said to the table. I thought of my chilly neighbors at my small apartment building in Dupont Circle in D.C., who pulled their Beamers and Jeeps into the garage and disappeared straight into their apartments. If I ran into them a block away, they'd walk right by me as if we'd never met. I then vowed that when I returned home, I'd break the ice by having my neighbors over for dinner.

To think that last week I'd banged on my ceiling with the end of a broom when my neighbor was vacuuming at midnight! "I could have been more tolerant," I told the table, "or waited to tell her that she'd woken me up when we next met in the hallway. Sustainability starts with people," I said in a tumble of words. I was surprised at the thoughts coming to the surface, but they felt like the truth. "We harm the planet because we don't feel a connection between our actions and the environmental impact," I finished.

"That's a great point," another man said. "Because in Mexico we have less, we live more sustainably. Most people in my town can't afford a car or an air conditioner, but we know everyone's name and look out for their children like they were our own." I remembered when I'd briefly lived in Israel during college, that my Israeli friends' neighbors barged into their homes without even knocking. Everyone was outspoken and direct, but at least they spoke from the heart and had a sense of community.

"What about our buildings in 2020?" our scribe put in, bringing us back on track. "I think they will be net generators of energy, with organic vegetable gardens on the roof." And off we went, spending thirty more invigorating minutes brainstorming our buildings of the future.

When our time was up and each table leader rose to present, I was amazed at the similarity of our visions. We were not the only group to dream of increasing community, of rebuilding neighborhoods out of the faceless sprawl of cities and suburbs, and of designing systems that would reduce our consumption and reconnect us with the earth.

I attended every session on sustainability I could find at the conference. By the end, my wallet was stuffed with business cards. As I walked back to my hotel I heard a buzzing in the air around me, like the hiss of a burning wick.

Something had changed in me. Unable to sleep that night again, I pulled out World Watch Institute's *State of the World 1992*, which I'd bought in D.C. and had yet to open, and read it from cover to cover. Once a year the Institute reviewed the environmental condition of the planet: food production, water resources, energy consumption, renewable production, population growth, species destruction, deforestation, and sustainable economics. It was all related to my industry—buildings.

Buildings, I learned, consumed 40 percent of our energy, 20 percent of our water, 40 percent of our wood. They contributed 20 percent of landfill waste. Poor air in buildings made people sick. Given that we spend 90 percent of our lives inside these giant boxes, this meant billions of dollars of lost productivity. After my years as a developer, I thought I knew a lot about buildings, but this was all new to me.

Suddenly, not knowing whether I'd been dreaming or awake thinking in the dark, I sat up and switched on the light. An astounding idea had come to me: I could make a difference in the world through sustainable buildings. Even though it was 3 A.M., I felt like getting up and devising a new game plan: Tomorrow already seemed too late. I went to the bathroom to splash some cold water on my face. Looking at my reflection as the water dripped down my forehead and cheeks, I felt the hugeness of the moment wash over me. This was what I wanted to do with my life. I made some notes on my pad, then went and stood at the window for a while, looking out at the wasteful lights of the sleeping city. When I finally climbed back under the covers, I hoped I could get some sleep and wake up with the sun. There wasn't a moment to lose. I had wasted too much of my life already.

CHAPTER 2

Florsheims to Ferragamos

I ARRIVED IN WASHINGTON, D.C., in September of 1982, twenty-two years old and a hotshot fresh out of Stanford. I'd majored in engineering management—a major that I'd designed, combining industrial and civil engineering coursework with a few business school classes. When I began hunting for jobs during my senior year, my cousin Diane invited me to work for her and offered to teach me the development business. I said yes instantly. She and her husband, Jim, were powerful figures in the real estate world, and their business was booming.

Jim and Diane shared a vast suite at 18th and L Streets downtown, with corner offices on opposite ends. Jim's office had a luxuriously thick beige and tan carpet and a huge mahogany desk that made him look powerful. Diane's had bleached white oak floors, lots of light, and pleasant touches such as an antique copper umbrella stand and a glass vase with tiger lilies that matched the hues of the Borofsky portrait hanging above them.

After my first few weeks in Washington, Diane called me into her office. "Gottfried, we have to do something about your wardrobe. It's a little, uh, Reaganite."

I looked down at my clothes, an off-the-rack navy blue suit, starched white shirt, and red tie. What was wrong with my wardrobe? "It's what everyone in D.C. is wearing," the salesman at May Company in Los Angeles had told me. But looking at Diane, dressed in a handsome black pantsuit, framed by her Italian glass desk and a backdrop of modern office buildings across the street, I had to admit it did feel a little stiff and cheap. Three days later, we were off to New York to go shopping.

At LaGuardia as we waited for our ride, the autumn air was crisp, hinting at winter. I pulled my red Stanford sweatshirt from my daypack and put it on.

Diane looked slim and elegant in a dark tailored wool skirt, an intricately woven gray sweater, and silk scarf. The Bottega Veneta purse was new, purchased in Paris on her fortieth birthday. She glanced at her gold Cartier watch and then reapplied her lipstick, though her thin lips were already perfectly glossed with thick red coats of Estée Lauder. "Jim, I thought you said he would be here at eleven." Her jaw clenched in irritation.

"George is reliable. I'm sure he's on his way," Jim answered easily. The face she turned to him was pinched. "You were going to wear the other jacket," she said. "It makes you look thinner." He *was* heavy, but I thought he looked dapper: black cashmere sweater, gray slacks, and tasseled burgundy shoes. A white hand-kerchief peeked from the pocket of his blue blazer. His black metal-framed glasses were by Emanuel Ungaro.

Taxis honked, and you could see the drivers' faces through the windows as they dreamed of other places—one hand on the wheel. Through this messy shuffle of yellows and blacks, Diane and Jim's ivory white limo slid to the curb as smooth as soap.

"Good morning, Mr. Katz. The Carlyle?" I had brought a sport coat specifically for the Hotel Carlyle, since Jim had told me they wouldn't serve you breakfast without one.

"Take us to Barney's first, George," Jim told the driver.

I'd heard of Barney's. Expensive. I had no savings, and my $2,000 paycheck was invariably gone by the end of the month. How could I afford to shop at Barney's?

My worries ballooned when the driver pulled up in front of the impressive seven-story building. Everything about the store seemed designed to intimidate me: its hulking size, the window displays of leather purses for men slung over the shoulders of haughty mannequins. Even the thin-faced door attendant, who stood staring blankly over our heads, made me feel inadequate. On the way in, I caught sight of the price tag on a black silk bathrobe: $1,550.

Once we'd entered, as I stood staring about me, a salesman appeared. He was groomed to the point of grotesqueness, his head and face shaved to the bone, save for an arrow-shaped patch below his bottom lip; black suit, black shirt, and a knife blade of a tie. Is that what he would make me look like?

"Your job is to deliver this California boy into vogue," Diane told him. "Let's start with suits." We went upstairs, with me trailing behind. I felt overwhelmed. The men's clothing, arrayed in Italian designer galleries, featured styles for all occasions. I imagined I'd need an Italian-English dictionary just to read the fabric care tags.

"How about Armani, or Hugo Boss?" the salesman asked. He seemed to be affecting an Italian accent, which, mixed with what sounded like Midwestern inflection, sounded strange, like an actor who couldn't quite get the accent down.

"No, that's not the right look for him," Diane said. The sales-man shut his mouth, cowed, no doubt, by her Chanel outfit and Bulgari gold necklace. She was so different from my mom, who still shopped at Loehmann's and sometimes wore Israeli beaded necklaces bought at the Temple's gift show. Yet they were first cousins, ten years apart in age, with the same roots in a small town in eastern Poland. "I used to change her diapers," my mother liked to say.

"He needs Versace," Diane told the salesman. Nobody asked me anything. I stood forgotten by a cascade of purple hued shirts. The last time I'd felt like this was on a shopping expedition with my mother—buying my Bar Mitzvah suit at Rudnick's in Beverly Hills.

The suits at the next boutique were strangely angular and V-shaped, with stiff shoulder pads. "Don't you think the shoulders are kinda puffy?" I asked, crushing the wedge of fabric in my fist. Falsies for men?

Diane ignored me; Jim was thumbing through stacks of shirts. As they flipped through assorted international silks in somber hues of black and gray, I retreated toward a rack of pants. Could I get out of this? No. I couldn't disappoint them. I wanted what they had, and if that meant wearing what they wore, then I would do that too. But, my God, the money!

"How about this?" Diane held up a dark blue and gray patterned suit.

"That's *gorgeous*," the salesman said as he helped me try on the jacket. "It complements his dark coloring."

"That looks great. Try on the pants," Jim said, slapping me on the shoulder.

"Here, try this one too." Diane lifted a medium-gray double-breasted suit with a thin, blue pinstripe off the rack. The huge lapels slanted down at a sharp angle, forming a V. It only had one button. At least I wouldn't have to remember which one to button.

I went to the dressing room and put the blue suit on. The smooth, lightweight wool felt very expensive. I looked at myself in the mirror. Black curly hair covered my ears above an open baby face. I stood straight, feeling taller than my height. I caught my own eyes as you might a stranger's, and admired myself. The college kid had vanished. I imagined myself shouting orders to my own limo driver: "Take me to the Ritz."

"Gottfried, I can't believe it's you," Jim cried when I emerged from the dressing room. "You look like a different man." He punched me in the chest.

"We'll take it," Diane said. "Jim, where should we have lunch? Do you think Turveau can take us at the Plaza?"

I'd turned the coat inside out looking for a price tag, with no luck. I knew it wasn't proper to ask, even if a single suit cost the same as the used VW Rabbit I'd just bought on credit.

"We'll take both suits," Diane said. The salesman put the suits on the counter and piled shirts and ties on them — two for each new suit, Hugo Boss, Zegna, Missoni. I had never seen patterns and colors like these on clothing, so modern and bold.

"Now, let's get rid of those Republican shoes," Diane said. I stared at my Florsheims, wanting to hide my feet somehow.

We trooped to the shoe department. "Try this," Diane said, handing me a beautifully sculpted but flimsy black slip-on. It was a Ferragamo. "These are beautiful," the salesman said as he brought me a size twelve. I slipped them on with ease. They were so light and soft — more like gloves than shoes. Though they were hard to walk in, I managed a slow shuffle and looked up at Diane for a reprieve. "They look great," Diane said. I wondered if they'd give any support on a construction job site.

A wave of heat spread across my face as I watched the total bill rise, item by item, at the cash register. The tally finished at $3,275. With each increase, it felt as if someone was incrementally shutting down my oxygen supply. I felt dizzy.

Jim glanced at my face. "Gottfried, don't worry, we're paying for the suits. You can buy the other things." He presented his platinum card to the salesman. I took a deep breath. I couldn't afford even the extras. I paused as if I'd forgotten my wallet. Then the sights and smells of the beautiful things in that room stormed my senses, and suddenly I didn't care. I handed over my credit card. It would take me months to pay off, but I was financing a new life.

CHAPTER 3

The Go-Go '80s

I'D SCORED MY OWN OFFICE just across the hall from Diane.
"What title should we give you?" she had asked me my first day as
we sat at the dark polished table in our small conference room.
Her hair was short. A flowered scarf was wrapped around her neck
and hung down her back. Framed photos of several of Jim's
recent buildings hung on the wall.

"One that gives me some authority," I answered, leaning back
in my chair, hands interlaced behind my neck. Three months
before, I'd been playing Ultimate Frisbee at Stanford, and now
here I was in a tailored suit with my own office, choosing a title. I
was twenty-two and full of beans. It all felt like play to me.

"How about Assistant to the President?" Diane said.

"Great!" The title linked me to Diane, who had all the power.

That day on my lunch hour, I went out and bought a leather
briefcase. It was from Britches, a Georgetown men's clothier. The
leather wasn't as fancy as Diane's jet-black eel-skin, but it was on
sale, and I could always replace it in a few months' time.

Life in D.C. was starting out just as my upbringing had led me
to expect it would. My father was a successful businessman, and I
grew up accustomed to the associated privileges: tennis lessons
and golf at Brentwood Country Club, a private plane, four years

at Stanford, the freedom to choose what I wanted to do with my life. This background provided me with a pedigree, an intimate knowledge of the pastimes and perks of the successful. The circles my father moved in were a web of money and connections I could rely on when the time came. His accomplishments groomed me for my own.

In our house when I was growing up, anything short of the highest achievement was flat-out unacceptable. Weekly progress reports, delivered at our Friday evening Shabbat dinners, helped ensure that my two brothers and I stayed on track. Attendance at these meals was mandatory.

"Richard, tell me the highlights of your week," Dad said to my brother at one such dinner, the table set with a beautiful white lace tablecloth. On top of it was a freshly baked challah, a kiddush cup filled with red wine, and the white Sabbath candles.

I snapped to attention, knowing my turn would come shortly. My hair was still wet from my shower. I'd spent the afternoon playing tennis at a friend's house, preparing for a weekend doubles tournament. I was fifteen.

My eldest brother, Rick, was eighteen and a senior at Pacific Palisades High School. His wavy hair was the color of rust, his body perfect. "I got an A on my English project for Mrs. O'Brien, and worked on my speech for graduation," he answered. "That's great, son. I'm proud of you." My dad reached over to touch Rick on the shoulder. Rick smiled, then rushed on, "Stanford sent me a large package on housing and course selection. I'm thinking maybe economics." He was a renaissance man: student body president, starting fullback on the football team, and headed to Stanford.

Dad pulled a pack of Newport cigarettes and a gold lighter from his pocket and lit up. "Judith, did you put the coffee up yet?"

Obediently, my mother put down her fork and went into the kitchen, clearing a few plates along the way. I found my mother beautiful, and at that time she looked several years younger than her forty-two years. Her looks were Semitic—thick dark hair, warm brown eyes, and olive skin—and revealed her European roots. Mom was always quiet at dinner, letting my father conduct the conversation. She was much different on the telephone with her mother or sister; they talked at the same time, sometimes even screaming at each other. They weren't angry; they simply wanted to be heard. The phone was a lifeline for my mom, pumping her with energy—especially when my dad retreated to his lounge chair in the living room to read his latest novel or flying journal.

"Glenn?" Glenn's head jerked up. As the second eldest, he was next—and Rick wasn't an easy act to follow. At sixteen, Glenn was heavy, but with a powerful build. He was in the tenth grade, a starting defensive tackle and All-State shot-putter. The academic side of school, however, did not especially captivate him at the time. "I guess I won't have to take you to visit colleges this summer," my father had said to Glenn one evening when, although he had a history test the next morning, Glenn had chosen to spend his time banging his drums to Led Zeppelin. That quiet remark was all Glenn needed to boost his grades from C's to A's within a couple of weeks.

Glenn now said, "I've been working on a new invention in the garage: a lighting system for my stereo. The lights vibrate with the beat of the music." He'd been down there all week, so engrossed in his project that Mom had to yell repeatedly when he had a phone call.

"What about your schoolwork? Did you have any tests this week?" Dad asked as he tapped his cigarette into the ashtray.

"In biology, yeah, uh, it didn't go too well," Glenn said to his plate.

"I can see where this is headed," Dad said. "I'll take it up with you later in your room." I watched Glenn pat our dog, Ginger, nervously under the table, but I had no time to feel sorry for him. I was up. I stiffened, readying myself for the inquisition. But instead, Dad started speaking about his own business. "I had a good day, I sold two contracts," he said. "The Gas Company asked us to help them groom their next president. That golf game last week with the chairman paid off." Dad was a management consultant, a leading expert in organizational strategy and computer systems, mostly dealing with Fortune 500 companies. My college education was paid by the preferred dividends he'd given us from his company.

"What was the other one?" Rick asked, always the dutiful son.

"Security Pacific wants us to supervise the design of their new computer center in Burbank. The contract is for $400,000."

My dad came to California after fleeing his father's furniture business in New York. Each year he would send Grandpa Lou his company's annual report. Although Dad's annual profit increased with each of his thirty years in business, the desired approval never came. After Grandpa Lou died, Dad went into a deep depression. He obtained emergency counseling. A month later, he was back to moving full speed ahead, with the brief break in his armor welded together again.

"David?" *Thump*. My throat swelled shut. Mom appeared at his elbow to pour him coffee. My heart beat fast, even though I had no reason to be worried. I rarely disappointed Dad. "Didn't you have an election?"

"Yes. I won." I had become the president of the Boy's League — a position held by both of my brothers before me. "I also got nomi-

nated for the Lion's Club Achievement Award." My class was graduating from junior high, and the award was based on our academic
and extracurricular achievements. I had worked hard and had
close to a 4.0 grade-point average to show for it. I was also on the
starting team of our football, baseball, and basketball teams. My
number of tennis trophies was growing. I'd been in student government since the seventh grade. In our family, all three—the grades,
the sports, and student government—were mandatory.

"That's wonderful," Dad said. As always, his praise soothed the
punched-stomach feeling, even motivated me to move on to the
next achievement.

The truth was, I wanted in: I wanted everything my father had,
and more. And now, in Washington, I felt that I had arrived. I had
built up my résumé by learning etiquette at the country club,
going to Stanford, and now I was apprenticing with Diane and
Jim. I wanted to skip the Motel 6's and head straight for the
Carlyle and the Ritz.

After I'd been with working for Diane for a year, I became a
project manager. We began to buy buildings and land that we
could improve through renovation and development. Mostly we
focused on urban infill: commercial office projects and rental
apartments. Our real estate projects were well located, designed
to meet market needs with an architectural statement, and finan-
cially well structured. However, Diane and Jim's real talent lay in
cultivating relationships within the power circles of Washington.
Through various connections, they'd get invited to high-society
parties and benefits where they met the wealthiest and most
important members of the establishment. Soon enough they'd be
striking deals, some worth millions, well before the properties hit

the market. "It's all about contacts," my father had said when I was interviewing for Stanford. "Your grades and extracurriculars are good, but it's well-placed letters of reference that'll get you in."

Diane and Jim's friends became business partners and vice versa. There were no boundaries, and the business never stopped, even on vacations. During one Saturday brunch at their house I witnessed Diane holding her own in a discussion of foreign policy over scrambled eggs with our ambassador to the UN, Jean Kirkpatrick. Diane read the *Wall Street Journal*, *Washington Post*, and *New York Times* every morning, and she subscribed to at least five financial and news magazines and the *New Yorker*.

One of our early investors was the Texas billionaire Robert Bass. Diane and Jim had met him through his chief architect, who had designed one of our earlier properties—a renovation of a historic mansion on Embassy Row.

On another project, I managed the leasing and then sale of one of Diane's early buildings in Arlington, Virginia. After the settlement, they handed me a $10,000 check—almost fifty percent of my starting salary! "Don't spend it all in one place," Diane said with a big smile. "You did a great job." After work that day I went and bought a new suit at Hugo Boss. When I got home, I called my folks with the good news, then pulled out a beer and toasted myself. I only wished I had a girlfriend to celebrate with.

As the deals closed, my net worth continued to increase. I was on my way, but with each step the triumphs needed to be bigger. I was following my father's plan, advancing faster than either of us thought possible, and yet the monetary buildup wasn't enough. So I channeled my energy into making more, and at a faster pace. "More is more" became my mantra.

I found out, though, that I still had an awful lot to learn.

One evening in October of that first year, Diane and I were kicking back on her couch at home. I was still living with them in their Georgetown house, sleeping in the top-floor guest room (though they'd had so many guests during the months I'd been there that I'd spent most nights bunking with their youngest son, Aaron). We'd just finished dinner, pasta and a salad prepared by their maid, which we'd followed up with Ben and Jerry's ice cream, three different flavors: Cherry Garcia, Chunky Monkey, and New York Fudge. Diane was flipping through magazines— U.S. News, Time, Forbes—as we watched the news, a recap of the Falkland Islands war. Jim sat next to her, looking at various construction magazines. Diane, as usual, looked great, even in jeans and a sweatshirt. On the wall in back of her was a large Helen Frankenthaler painting featuring masses of flowing orange and turquoise paint. They owned two of her best-known paintings; the other one was on a museum tour.

Diane looked up from her magazine and studied me for a minute. Then she said, "David, I don't like what I've been hearing about you around the office." Jim muted the television, but I kept staring at the anchorman's face. Had I heard her correctly? I'd thought everything was going well as I eased into working a regular job.

"What do you mean?" I asked. I was panting a little. What could she have heard?

"You've been using the computer in accounting without asking permission. And you don't address Keith Silver as 'mister.' He's our client, and much older than you. You should show respect."

I shrank into the couch cushions. But she wasn't finished. "You question everything I tell you." She said that when I'd run some numbers on a real estate deal I argued when she tried to tell me I'd made a mistake. "You have to learn to pay your dues. And to understand that I sign your paycheck. I am your cousin, and will always love you, but keep it up and I'll send you back to California." Her glasses reflected an image from the TV, a spaceship careening through a field of stars, out of control. It was a preview for Spielberg's new movie, E.T.

I stared at the ornate white ceiling trim, focusing on a particular spot but not seeing it. Who was she to scold me? Was I a child? I got up abruptly and went outside, walking past the covered pool, white lounge chairs, and a patio umbrella covered with leaves. My hands were cold in my pockets, but my face was hot. I could hear traffic on Wisconsin Avenue. The yard was deep in leaves fading from rich red and yellow to dry and brittle brown. For the first time that fall I could see my breath.

I relaxed a notch. I was Diane's young second cousin, just a kid really, and I'd been running around her company as if I was one of the owners. No one had taught me how to be a good employee—to patiently work my way up the ladder. The family-dinner "board meetings" with my dad and brothers and my Stanford case studies had taught me to understand business only from the perspective of the boss. I flinched at the image that appeared in my mind: me arriving home in disgrace, my dad waiting at the airport gate, disappointment etching his face below his Reno Air Races cap and glasses. I went back in the house. "I'm sorry," I said. "I'll do better."

The next morning, I rose at six and was the first one at the office. It was the first time I had to use my key and enter the alarm code. I later went upstairs and apologized to Mary, the person responsible for the computer, and gave her flowers. She thanked me, and soon became a friend and office ally. "Don't worry about me for dinner," I said to Diane later that day, as she and Jim headed home. "I'm going to work late." Jim nodded. Diane smiled.

I was a new man—and more important, a new employee. I tried to make myself indispensable by typing up the notes I took at the weekly management meetings that I attended with Diane, and by meticulously tracking follow-up tasks for us both. I wrote up weekly status reports on my work, prioritizing the pending items. In short, I worked toward new goals: humility and patience.

No sooner had I won Diane's confidence back, though, than I was faced with a new problem: trying to keep people from guessing how lost I often was. My cousins' trust frequently catapulted me into situations where I had to play catch-up—and fast. I did a lot of sweating in those days, put in a lot of late nights cramming for meetings with people who had twice my years and ten times my experience. When I found myself out of my depth, I redoubled my efforts.

Once, early on, Diane and Jim (who were off in Europe) asked me to negotiate a lease with a prospective architect tenant for a building we'd recently purchased in Georgetown, on Wisconsin Avenue. When I arrived at the meeting, I encountered ten men, most of whom had gray hair and had spent several decades working as architects and real estate brokers. It was a rainy day and dark in the conference room, which was made even gloomier by dark wood paneling. I tried to look calm despite the pangs of panic in my stomach. It was my first lease negotiation. I was twenty-four—the same age as many of these men's children, I imagined. I hoped my new suspenders and matching bow tie made me look older.

"Who represents the building owner?" asked the man from the architecture firm, Perkins & Will.

Our leasing broker, Steve Goldstein, pointed at me. I shifted in my seat. "David Gottfried," I said.

"Do you have the authority to negotiate on behalf of the building owners?" he asked with surprise. I realized he thought I was a junior assistant to one of the other men. He gathered his papers as if he was going to leave. Everyone looked around uneasily.

For a moment I froze, feeling a dumb remark waiting to escape my mouth. I looked from face to face, my mind blank except for a humming sound. I was glad I'd worn an undershirt, because I could feel the sweat running down my back. And then, I found my voice. "Do you think I would have called this meeting if I intended to waste your time? I'm here to negotiate a deal. Shall we proceed, or should I lease the space to someone else?" (We had no other interested parties.) The room went silent.

Their broker cleared his throat. "Where should we begin?" he asked. I noticed his cufflinks, brilliant white-gold squares. The lead architect picked up his copy of the lease.

Encouraged, I sat back in my chair and launched the opening salvo. "My understanding is that we don't yet have agreement on the base rental rate. What are you willing to pay?"

The principal put on his glasses and looked at his notes. "We can't pay more than $17.50 a square foot," he said.

The negotiations were in motion now—though, at first, I felt like a player in a ping-pong match. I was getting the ball on the table every time, but remained unsure whether I could handle the return if my opponent hit the ball with a spin. Heads in the room swiveled from me to the principal and back again. I wondered what the score was.

Then the broker entered the discussion, and I addressed his questions firmly and easily. Soon I found myself relaxing, even enjoying myself. I could do this. In the end—the negotiations went on for over an hour—I pushed as hard as possible without killing the deal. I did make some concessions, but all at levels within my authorized parameters.

"You were fantastic." Steve patted me on the shoulder after everyone had left. "You can work with me anytime." Back on the sidewalk, I jumped up and slapped a No Parking sign. *Bang!* I'd nailed the deal. I was on the verge of skipping to my car when I noticed a woman looking at me and smiling invitingly, taking in the suit, the tie, and the confidence. She wasn't looking at me as a kid in a suit, but as a man, a D.C. power broker, a big shot—and I felt like one. I returned her smile, curbing the urge to skip.

Over the next year, I went on to lease all of the Georgetown building's vacant office space, plus its thirty-five apartments. I also supervised the design and build-out of the tenant improvements. Jim's firm did the construction work. I enjoyed learning how to read blueprints and walking the space as it came into being. After the project was finished, I made a long list of items that needed touch-up—called a "punch list." I'd manage completion of those items as if my life depended on it.

Our overall leasing numbers were higher than projected, and that increased the value of the property. Falling interest rates increased our return even more. After a year, we refinanced, trading our construction loan into a larger permanent loan and pulling out the difference tax free.

I was awarded a small ownership interest in the building. When Diane later handed me my first partnership distribution, I opened the envelope to find a check for $30,000—more money than I'd ever possessed. I hugged her. "Now you're on your way," she said, then added, with a twinkle in her eye, "That's still only ten decent suits at Barneys."

We bought properties in D.C., northern Virginia, and Maryland, everything from agricultural land to office buildings and large multifamily apartment communities. Diane and her new partner, Harry Gold, gave me a 2 to 3 percent ownership interest in each. "What's the value of the property?" I'd ask Diane after we closed each deal, and then I'd calculate the increase in my personal net worth. Some of the deals added over $100,000 to my paper wealth. My bank account also grew. I dreamed of hitting a million before my thirtieth birthday.

As a property owner, I also received tax shelter benefits from property depreciation write-offs. None of us had to pay income taxes, and that made our salaries and the distributions tax free. I was surprised at how easy the game was. I thought it was normal.

Before President Reagan changed the tax laws in 1986, many developers were putting together real estate investment deals called syndications, aimed at high tax bracket professionals. These investors were allocated a majority of a project's tax losses in return for a cash investment. Even if the development didn't make money, the investor achieved a high rate of return from the tax shelter. And the developers got the cash they needed. I took an exam in 1985 on the securities laws and broker-dealer requirements, and we formed our own real estate syndication company called D.C. Securities. My new business cards identified me as Vice President. Harry Gold's top financial officer, Larry, was the president. His deal-structuring capabilities were incredible, and I meticulously studied every financial pro forma he prepared, even reviewing the calculation formulas on my IBM PC. He and I exchanged files through our newly purchased Hayes smart modems. Before the Internet and digital communications, the transfers took hours (operating at only 300 bits per second versus 1.3 million for DSL).

We began to buy and fix up buildings. As a full project manager, I was in charge of the day-to-day work flow, managing a team of outside experts: lawyers, contractors, and architects; leasing agents, appraisers, vendors, and property managers. I loved being a developer. It fit me better than my old Stanford sweatshirt ever did. Taking charge seemed natural to me, especially with my father's authoritative voice guiding me from within. It was obvious to me now, that I was prewired for success.

As deal followed deal, Diane and Jim lived life "big." "You can't take it with you when you're dead," Jim liked to say. They bought a house that looked like a castle in Bethesda, Maryland. The outside was ivy-covered red brick, the inside cool, with exposed brick and masonry walls. I never did get to all the rooms on its four floors. They installed their own finishes—carpeting, wall covering, a new kitchen, and window treatments. The fourteen-foot-high floral living-room drapes alone cost $100,000. In the backyard an English landscaped rose garden led down to a black-bottomed swimming pool.

I began to view my cousins' assets as part mine. It gave me great pride to let myself into their house with my own key, or borrow Diane's Mercedes convertible when they were out of town. Diane and Jim traveled twelve weeks a year, so they had to delegate responsibility. Despite my youth, I became their most trusted eyes. I attended charity functions on their behalf, was made a trustee for their children, and was first on the security company call list—and more than once was awakened in the middle of the night by a false alarm and had to sprint over to their house to inspect. Having that kind of authority and responsibility at age twenty-four was amazing—and addicting.

They made Martha's Vineyard their haven, renovating a big old house on a bluff overlooking the water, just down the road from the lighthouse. It had three levels and a full guest cottage for the hired help. On the top was a cupola built as a lookout, to watch for the island's infamous whaling ships. The best feature was a six-foot-tall fireplace made of large ballast found on the island.

"Come on, Gottfried, it's time to go," Diane would say to me many a Friday afternoon during the summer. An hour later, I'd be seated aboard the jet they co-owned with several friends. Private planes were as comfortable for me as cars are for most people, since I'd grown up flying everywhere in my father's plane. If an automobile journey took more than two hours, we would fly instead. My father was then on his sixth plane, an eight-seat pressurized twin-engine Cessna 421 Golden Eagle. His airplane had changed our lives. Each year, as a family we took several flying trips all over the country: national parks, dude ranches, unpopulated parts of Mexico, and skiing and fishing trips. I looked at Diane and Jim's jet—a Falcon—with an appraising eye. I hoped that soon I'd have my own.

"David, why don't you start collecting?" Jim asked one afternoon as we investigated an antique shop on the quaint Vineyard main street. Their house contained dozens of collectables: craftworks, ceramics, paintings, model ships, old telescopes and compasses, scrimshaw sculptures, baskets, and handmade quilts. I began timidly to buy some items, mostly as gifts—a porcelain vase for my mom and hand-painted china plates for a friend's wedding.

Many of my cousins' friends and acquaintances on the island were high-society types. "David, come meet our mayor," she said to me one afternoon on a friend's deck. On another occasion, we were invited to take an afternoon cruise with a New York real estate mogul on his 110-foot yacht. I counted a crew of seven, complete with personal chef. The master suite had a marble bathroom and Jacuzzi. I overheard that they had spent $10 million for the ship's renovations. As I lay on the teak deck in a chaise longue, I lifted up my Heineken beer and toasted Jim.

By the time I was twenty-six and had been with the company four years, the economy was in full swing, with each of our deals adding up to an increasing personal net worth. There were times when what we were doing felt as if it should be illegal, like not having to pay income taxes, making $500,000 on a deal concluded over roast quail and vintage merlot, or watching the value of a property quadruple after a very modest renovation, minimal landscaping, and putting our company name on the sign out front. It seemed so easy if you ran in the right circles. I never considered development to be shameful, or felt that I was compromising my integrity. After all, we treated our employees and tenants well and gave to charity. My cousins were enormous donors—to all types of causes (health, the Jewish community, arts and education). They'd donated their time to the construction of the new Holocaust museum to be built on the Mall.

By 1987, at age twenty-six, I had enough money to bankroll my own real estate development company. I felt terrible about leaving Diane's company, but I needn't have worried. Diane and Jim not only wished me well, but threw me a big party and gave me a gold and silver Cartier watch. Its luster seemed to mirror the good fortune that we'd had over the past four years together.

I set up a small office under the name Gottfried Development, Inc. I thought the title of owner and president fit me perfectly, and sent out announcements with a picture of Stonehenge on them. Then I began looking for redevelopment projects, using my association with Diane and Jim to provide me credibility with the brokerage and banking community.

In short order I found investors: the principal, Brian Lash, a wealthy doctor, was a longtime friend of Diane and Jim's. He and two well-to-do buddies said that they would back me if I found a good property. I loved driving around suburban Maryland, D.C., and northern Virginia looking for potential development projects. In late 1987 I found a fifty-thousand-square-foot, twenty-year-old office building in Arlington, Virginia, on Columbia Pike, not far from the Pentagon. The three-story building was run down, but the lead tenant, Control Data Learning Center, had just renewed its lease for five years. As a condition of purchase with the owner, I agreed to renovate Control Data's space before settlement. Jim agreed to perform the $200,000 worth of work, deferring payment until I closed the purchase in February 1988.

The building needed a full renovation and leasing of about one-third of the space, which was vacant and in need of upgrade. My financial model predicted that it would then start making money. However, my partners and I had decided to finance the upgrades with a second loan that would use up the increased cash flow after we were fully occupied. That provided higher leverage, which would increase our return, but also our risk if we didn't achieve full occupancy.

"I want into the deal," my dad surprised me by saying one evening, on the phone. "Can you carve out a limited-partner piece for me?" I didn't reply for what seemed like an hour. I wanted my father to be part of my success and loved sharing my triumphs with him, but I was afraid of having him involved. What if the deal didn't work out? Would it impair our relationship? Would he try to influence my decisions as the managing general partner of the new partnership we'd set up to buy the building? In the end, Dad invested $135,000 in the building for a 20 percent stake. Brian and his two partners were excited to have him in the deal, as it lessened their cash requirement, but they cosigned on the loan with me and became co–general partners. At his request, Dad's only risk was his investment, and he became our sole limited partner.

"What do you think?" I asked my parents, as the building filled the windshield of my new BMW 325. It was six months since I'd purchased the property. "I know it doesn't look like much, but I'm going to renovate it." I had on my Versace double-breasted suit. My dad was in the front seat, and my mother in the back. He wore a thick gold bracelet on his right wrist, the one he always told me he could use to buy his way home with from anywhere in the world in case of trouble. Around his neck, he'd also begun wearing a gold chain with *chai*, the Hebrew word for life, dangling from it.

"What part of it is mine?" my dad asked. He peered out the window at the boxy and unattractive 1960s office building. Seeing it through his eyes, I noticed that the blue tiles on the façade were falling off, leaving white gaps. Mounted to the building was a big sign that said Control Data Learning Center; the lights were burnt out. Sprinklers watered the bare lawn; dirt spilled onto the sidewalk. I looked over at him but couldn't read his expression.

"The third floor," I said. My other partners and I split the rest.

"Is that all I get for $135,000?"

"Ira, be nice," my mother said, wagging her finger at him. "The building has great potential."

I parked the car in the rear and walked them to the front of the building, up the cracked concrete stairs with its twenty-year-old yellow banister, and into the lobby. It was spacious, with an old speckled yellow polished terrazzo floor and a small directory of the tenants near the old hydraulic elevator. I pointed out the listing on the bottom: "Management by Gottfried Development, Inc., Suite 306." I smiled broadly.

We took the elevator to the third level. "Our new carpet and paint colors," I pointed out in the hallway. The walls were white, the carpet a purple salt-and-pepper pattern; the door of each tenant suite was adorned with a new gray sign. "Very nice," my mother said. "The carpet is a good choice. It won't show dirt." She bent to touch the new flooring. "Right, Ira?" She looked up. My father had walked off ahead. He stopped and straightened an exit light, then walked over to a fire extinguisher and looked at its tag. "You should have someone check all of these," he said. "This one is expired." I was transported right back to the dining room table when he would inspect my homework, focusing mostly on the spelling and grammar errors. "*Relevant* is spelled *a*-n-t," he'd say as I cringed.

"This is my office," I said, opening the door. "I did the design and supervised the construction." The small suite smelled of fresh paint and new carpet.

"Good layout, very efficient," my father said, glancing in and then making his way to the end of the hallway. He knocked lightly on the walls and opened and closed doors, making faces. I couldn't tell if he disapproved of the building's construction or was frustrated that he couldn't find anything wrong.

"The art is very nice," my mother said. I had picked up posters during one of my New York trips and had them displayed in a black metal frame. "We're so proud of you, son." She beamed and put her arm around me, giving me a squeeze. But I was looking at my father.

"What do our other partners think?" Dad asked. "They sure got a good deal." He straightened a picture.

"They're already talking about buying more buildings together." I smiled and looked for a reaction. Would he want in?

"And how's the leasing going?" The man was thorough.

"I've already leased about 85 percent of the building. At rents higher than we projected."

At last Dad smiled. "I'm proud of you, Son. I always knew you had it in you," he said, and I almost crumpled to the floor. I had wanted so desperately to hear those words, I felt exhausted from the long wait.

CHAPTER 4

Her Dress Was the
Color of Money

ALTHOUGH I'D MADE LOADS OF MONEY as a junior partner
of Diane's company, and now was running my own development
company, it wasn't enough. I wanted to climb even higher—but I
didn't know how. I didn't have enough capital to buy bigger
buildings than the one in Arlington. I'd looked at dozens, and
even placed deposits on a few, but at the end of the study periods
I'd always backed out. Now it was 1989 and the economy was
declining; the prospect of investing was becoming less appealing.

One day, the phone rang. I was in my office in the Control
Data building, wolfing a pancetta and mozzarella sandwich. On
the line was Karen Cohen, the chief counsel of a billionaire
friend of Diane's. Karen was managing Z Development. I shook
my head, not sure I was hearing right: Z Development was the
talk of the town, and they wanted to interview *me* to be their head
of real estate. We set up a meeting for that evening: 8 P.M. at her
apartment.

Although I thought that was strange—why not meet at the
office?—I hung up the phone, ecstatic. I knew that others, with
decades more experience than I, were jockeying for the position.
One was a senior partner in a prominent law firm. Karen, though,
said they'd heard great things about me from Diane: that I was

loyal, bright, and very thorough; that without me her company would not be half what it was; that she couldn't bear to see me go when I'd left to start my own firm. Diane had not only managed to make me into one of the hottest up-and-comers in the D.C. industry, but she'd also convinced a billionaire she was doing her a favor in recommending me!

This firm had an international reputation and endless cash. As the economy dropped, companies were contracting, but Z Development stayed in the market buying. Recently it had purchased two properties in northern Virginia, with a total development potential of over five million square feet—for cash. No one had ever done that, at least not for $50 million. One property was located along the freeway to Dulles Airport; the other had over five hundred acres zoned commercial: it was the size of a golf course community or a small city. Now it was looking as if I could be part of that empire building, and at no personal risk.

That evening I hopped in the shower and then shaved for the second time that day, cutting myself in my hurry. It was already 7:30.

As I stripped the plastic from a laundered shirt, my eye fell on the ring of keys on my bureau. They opened every door in the Control Data building, which was now fully leased at double the rental rates when we'd first bought the building. I picked up the keys and felt their reassuring weight in my hand. Taking a new job, I thought, would mean closing my company and letting go of everything I had worked for. Even though I'd only bought one building so far, I was pursuing my dream. All my life I had envisioned owning my own company. "You need to be your own boss," my father had drilled into my brothers and me.

I put the keys down and went to the living room. Twelve-foot-high floor-to-ceiling windows looked out over a small rear parking

lot. The white walls were covered with black-and-white photo-
graphs I'd taken while a student at Stanford, and framed Rothko
posters from the New York Museum of Modern Art. A long glass-
top dining table stood in the middle of the room surrounded by
six matte and rounded black metal chairs, a porcelain bowl from
Martha's Vineyard resting in the center. I stood next to my new
black leather couch, buttoning my shirt. I'd bought all the furniture in my apartment in one day from Uzolo on Connecticut
Avenue. Most of it came from Italy. The overstuffed sofa chair
took six weeks to arrive. I'd spent $1,200 on the ottoman alone. It
may have been their biggest sale ever, I had thought more than
once. A Toshiba VCR, a super-high-band unit with built-in editing, sat in a glass case under the Sony TV. On the other side of
the room was a complete stereo system by Bose with six-foot
Duntech Sovereign speakers in Brazilian rosewood.

My hurry forgotten, I dropped on the couch to think about the
impending interview. This was the big leagues—working for billionaires. The telephone rang. It was Diane. "Play it cool," she
said. "This is important. Don't act like a big shot; you're too young.
I've told them great things about you, so play your cards right."

I flushed, disliking being lectured as if I were a child, but I
owed Diane. "I know. I'll try."

"Don't commit to anything less than $150,000, be elusive, ask
for ownership points on all company projects," Diane continued
doggedly, "and if you feel as if anything dodgy is going on, get
out and come back to us." She said she'd heard a couple of unsa-
vory rumors, but then there were rumors about every company.
"Probably just other firms jealous about Z Development's capital," she said. I told her I'd be careful.

The musky scent of my cologne rose to my nostrils. I had put on Azzaro, bought during my last trip to Paris—it was Jim's favorite. I always used it before going out on a date. (Although I was constantly dating, few relationships lasted longer than three months.) After my shower I'd slapped some on each cheek. It made me feel more alive. Then I caught myself. What was I doing? This was a job interview, not a date. But I'd heard that Karen was single and striking. Why not do something a little extra?

Traffic was busy on the four-lane road leading into the west end of town. I parked my car on M Street and walked around the corner to 22nd. Karen's apartment building was on the corner. It had a restaurant next door; I watched as a couple paused to study the menu posted in the window.

The door buzzed and I went in. Karen was on the top floor, the penthouse. I took the elevator up. She opened the door at my first knock, extending her hand, and I was immediately glad I'd worn the cologne. She had green eyes set in rich, lightly freckled skin; her thick and flowing black hair, loosely twisted, hung midway down her back. She wore a low-cut, tight green silk dress. No bra. I smelled a strong, sensual perfume, underneath which her scent was musty, almost as if she hadn't used deodorant. I liked the strong smell. She stood close to me and her seductive body emanated a heat that was at once magnetic and disconcerting.

I took her hand and she led me into the apartment. A dozen designer pots and pans hung from a rack in her open kitchen. Flowing drapes hid the windows, while oriental rugs covered the polished wood floor. There were antiques from the Far East and Africa and several oil paintings of flowers. I winced at the thought of the framed museum posters back in my sparse apartment.

Imagining a Borofsky hanging in my own home, I hoped I soon could afford original art like my cousins had.

"Wine?" Karen asked. I sat down awkwardly on a white leather couch adorned with small silk pillows. A bottle of chilled chardonnay stood already open on the coffee table, two crystal glasses next to it. They looked like ones I'd seen at Tiffany when I went there for the first time with Diane. One hundred fifty dollars each.

"Sure, why not?" My voice came out high and nervous. She poured some wine, picked up the glasses, and, smiling, joined me on the couch. I felt a mix of caution and excitement. This was a damn strange interview.

"To the future." Karen clicked her glass against mine. She looked at me expectantly.

"To the future." I tried to smile. "So, where are you from?" I asked nervously.

"I grew up in New York, but my parents are from Israel. I went to college at Columbia and law school at NYU. I came to D.C. for this job. How about you?" she asked. "New York?" Her nipples looked erect under her dress.

"Los Angeles."

"Mmm. Beach boy. And are you seeing someone?"

"What?" I gulped wine to cover my surprise. "No, I broke up with my last girlfriend about a year ago." In my mind I saw the boxes stacked in the lobby of a young—and, as it turned out, very insecure—woman I'd lived with for a few months, an experience unpleasant enough to make me lose my nerve when it came to relationships.

"I'm sorry," Karen said. She didn't look sorry.

"How about you?" I asked. She seemed the type to play the field, even have an affair with a married man or two. "I've been taking a breather. But I'm thinking it's time to get back in the game." She reached for my wine glass. "More?" I nodded, though I was already feeling the effect of the first glass on my empty stomach.

She poured more for us both. "Let me show you our plans for the properties." She pointed at the blueprints spread out on the dining room table.

We spent the next three hours reviewing the drawings and discussing the company's development history and plans. Both seemed like a mess to me. They'd overpaid for the properties, buying them at the height of the market. For many firms this would mean ruin, but from all appearances, Z Development could afford to ride it out.

"Are you interested?" Karen asked when we'd finished. She looked me in the eye.

Not precisely sure what she was referring to, I cleared my throat. "I'm making a lot of money running my own business. I'd have to give that up, close my office."

"Just tell me what it will take," she said.

"One hundred fifty thousand base salary," I said, "plus equity in the projects, for starters." My voice deepened. I was comfortable talking business.

"We can manage something close to that," Karen said. Silent for a moment, she glanced away, then back at me. She learned across the table toward me. "Do you think we'll get involved?" My knee jolted involuntarily forward, almost knocking over my glass. Not knowing what to say, I just smiled.

I drove home along 22nd Street toward Dupont Circle. It was 11 P.M. and few cars were on the road. Despite the hour, it felt early. I called my dad in L.A. on my new $2,500 cellular car phone to tell him about my entrée to the big leagues. I didn't mention the electric charge between Karen and me. "Great, but don't get your hopes up, Son," he said. "The deal hasn't been inked yet." I then drove to a diner on Connecticut Avenue and celebrated by bolting down a burger, fries, and chocolate shake.

The meeting with Karen's boss, Yvonne, went well. She hired me at twice the salary I'd made working with Diane. I closed my office, letting my secretary go and hiring a friend to manage the Control Data building. Brian and the other two partners were upset that I wouldn't be available to oversee the daily management and buy more properties with them. I knew I was letting them down but decided not to think about it. This was such an enormous opportunity.

Over the next few weeks Karen and I worked obsessively on the firm's two real estate development projects. I spent my first weekend with the company reading all the files she'd assembled since the inception of Z Development. "I can't believe your level of detail," Karen said. "I never really look at these things too closely." The next week I drew up a strategic plan for the company. I was eager to prove myself.

"Good work," Yvonne said to me the following week, at a lunch at the Four Seasons with the three of us. (Yvonne lived in San Francisco with her lawyer husband and paid monthly visits to D.C., where she owned another house—as she did in London and the south of France.) My memo had advised the company to hold off on construction while the market recovered, except for digging the holes for the foundations, which would prevent the property's zoning permits from expiring. Before this, they had been planning to proceed full speed ahead—straight into a down market, which would have caused them to lose millions.

Yvonne leaned forward and put her hand on my arm. Her strong perfume, beautiful smile, and European accent aroused me. "What a catch you are," she said. I wiped my lips with my napkin to hide my pleased grin.

For the first few months we continued renting office space in an executive suite just around the block from Karen's apartment. But since the properties were in northern Virginia, we decided for political reasons to move into our own office space in Reston. For the first time my apartment was really far from work. Karen supervised the design and construction of the new office—double the space we needed, especially for just two employees and an assistant. The firm and its owners had great wealth, but they lacked staff and a business infrastructure. That was why they'd hired me—to help build it up.

The finished office looked like a designer's showroom. Karen and Yvonne had gone on a shopping spree for new art and fancy dishware for our kitchen. "Which marble do you like for your desk?" Karen asked me one day as we toured the space during its construction. I never dreamed that I would have a custom desk. "How about a brown leather couch and matching chair?" She showed me a brochure from Herman Miller. They must have dropped $40,000 on my office alone. Once we moved in, we had fresh flowers brought in weekly. "It's just lovely," Yvonne said during her first visit. "Let's have some tea to celebrate." It was served on the newly bought china from Tiffany.

I spent my workday with Karen—or rather, being dropped in on by her. Even when I shut my door for privacy, within minutes Karen would interrupt to ask me something.

Occasionally she would catch me on my way out at the end of the day and invite me over for dinner, saying she wanted to continue a discussion we'd been having about one of our projects. "Can't today. Really stressed. Maybe next week," was my typical response. Afraid of getting involved, I was fighting for my independence.

After a month of working together, however, I ran out of excuses and did go over for dinner. She kept the red wine flowing. "I've had enough," I said at one point. The alcohol was soaking in, and I was afraid of losing control. I was sitting on the couch, my right hand a balled fist. I didn't like to be pushed, even by a seductive woman.

"Oh, come on," she urged and poured me another glass. Then she picked up her own glass and walked into the bedroom. She didn't return. I waited. Her door was partway open. I kept looking over at it, but I didn't hear anything. Had she gone to sleep? "Karen?" I called. Nothing.

I walked over to the door. I still didn't hear anything. My pulse accelerated. Should I go home? I felt weak and a little drunk.

I pushed open the door. "What took you so long?" she said from the bed where she lay naked. I felt a jolt of blood hit my veins as my heartbeat accelerated. I went over and embraced her. A musky cloud of desire rose off her, and it took hold of me. She reached for my belt buckle, and then my pants. Soon I too stood naked.

I pushed her down on the bed and climbed on top of her. We kissed, as our hands explored. Like a volcanic eruption, the tension of the past month flowed out of us. The line between work and play had never been all that distinct with Karen anyway. It felt natural to sleep with her; she was a sexual creature.

I stayed the night. Karen snored lightly at my side as I stared at the ceiling, squirming against the dampness of the sheets. I felt greasy and confused.

For the next few months, Karen wanted to see me all the time, and we spent many evenings at her apartment. Sometimes we would travel for business, usually to New York, where we man-aged an office building owned by Yvonne in midtown. Karen liked the best hotels. Once we stayed at the Peninsula on Fifth Avenue, courtesy of the business.

Karen pushed our developers and architects hard, often asking them to do one thing, then changing her mind. One time, she asked our development consultant to create a financial spread-sheet for one of our buildings, giving him a short deadline, which meant his staff was forced to work all night long. When we met to review the numbers, however, she exploded: "You got it all wrong. You didn't include the carry costs for the properties since we bought them. Do it again, and I'd also like to see graphs of the fig-ures." In fact, he had created the charts, but she didn't notice. On another occasion she hired a prominent architect to do some ren-derings for a new building. "Is that all you have?" she snapped when he came to our offices to present his drawings. "If so, we won't need your services anymore."

Karen withheld information when she deemed it necessary. Once, even though she knew she was going to fire a consultant, she put him on a huge project, only to terminate him right in the middle, when the project was far enough along that we could manage it ourselves. She leaned on our contractors for confiden-tial information about other firms they worked for. She loved to show up late to meetings. "Let them wait," she'd say with a wave of her hand. Her manner disturbed me.

Moreover, there was something decadent about the way Z Development was run. It bled money on unsound deals, throwing lavish parties, leasing fancy cars, and allowing very loose account-ing on executive spending accounts; yet Karen would squeeze every penny out of the architects, cut corners on construction, and renege on contracts, even though the attorney fees for doing so would sometimes cost more than simply paying off the con-tracts. Karen had been a litigator before coming to Z Development. Like a mother tiger with claws extended, she loved fights and was always the first to lash out.

I was not used to this. "I've always run a clean show," my father often said while I was growing up. "I've been audited several times, and was complimented each time by the IRS auditor on how neatly I ran my business."

Once when I was sixteen — I had just gotten my license and my parents were out of town — I borrowed my father's new Mercedes to drive it to school. I underestimated the width of the car while parking. When I pulled into the space, the fender got wedged under the adjacent car. In my panic, I put the car into reverse and pushed on the gas. I heard a loud ripping noise as the fender tore away. "Shit! Shit! Shit!" I yelled. My pulse shot through the roof. I stopped the car, got out, and, for ten minutes, sat on the curb and threw rocks as hard as I could into the nearby hillside. Then I walked over to the principal's office. He came out with me to look at the cars. "You really did a job on her, huh?" he said, shaking his head. We went back to his office and he called a towing service, while I sat in a chair across from him shivering.

My parents didn't return home for several days. I was afraid to tell my brothers, and couldn't eat or sleep. What would my father do to me? Endless scenarios ran through my head, none of them pretty. I lost five pounds; rings formed under my eyes. The end-less waiting felt like its own prison sentence.

When Dad got home, I showed him the car. "This will cost you a year of allowance. You'll also have to work it off," he said. The fender was shredded, and there was a deep gouge in the passenger door. He was pale and stood with fists clenched. I'd greatly disap-pointed him, and for months he considered me untrustworthy.

I never forgot that experience. He'd told me to never touch his car, yet I'd driven it to school as a thrill, to push the edge. The incident taught me at a young age that I wasn't built for lying, cheating, or stealing.

The way Karen treated people meant there was always an undercurrent of distrust with our outside design and development team. She made a lot of enemies in Washington, to the point that people sometimes refused to work with us. I was part of a group people didn't want to associate with, and it felt horrible.

One day at work, as I reviewed the financials for one of our development projects, Karen came into my office and shut the door. She had a mischievous grin on her face. "What's up?" I asked. She raised a red-polished fingernail to her lips.

As I watched, pen frozen in my hand, she unbuttoned her blouse, then slipped out of her skirt. She walked over to my desk, hopped up, and leaned over to kiss me. "Do you want to play?" I scooted my chair back a bit and sat frozen, as if a cobra were on my desk, coiled and ready to strike. "Oh come on, don't you want to have some fun?" I was silent. I considered my office sacred space, and felt violated.

She didn't notice. She slid over to my side of the desk and eased herself onto my lap. Everything—well, almost every-thing—in me resisted what was about to happen. At the same time, I was a young man, and I got excited. When she reached out to embrace me, I tried to push her away. She made a move to kiss me, and I turned my head. Finally, though, I couldn't hold back any longer: I kissed her back and let her push me back on my chair. As the climax built, so did my self-loathing. I was being seduced—and in my own office. Afterward, when Karen had left, I was disgusted to see the damp outline of my body in the leather chair.

After that encounter with Karen I felt empty, as if that climax had drained me. I sat through meetings without hearing a word and stopped going to the gym. For the first time my work didn't captivate me, and in negotiations I felt like a boxer pounding on an undermatched opponent, fighting just for the money.

At night I looked through boxes of stuff I'd brought to D.C. and never unpacked. I listened to a bunch of old tapes—Paul Simon, Carol King, the Eagles—and paged through some textbooks I'd kept from Stanford. In one box I found a portfolio of prints from the last photography class I'd taken. I spread them on a table on top of some papers I'd been ignoring. Taken in San Francisco's Chinatown, they were still inspiring. I'd mimicked the printing style of Yousuf Karsh, with strong shades from blackest black to stark white. Seeing the photos made me realize how much I'd changed, and how much I'd lost. I had crossed a dozen lines of the ethics that Dad had ingrained in my two brothers and me. As I sank deeper, I began to withhold information from him and from Diane and Jim. I was embarrassed. At a physical, the doctor asked me if I was depressed—my blood pressure was high and I'd put on weight. I had trouble looking him in the eye and responded evasively. I'd become the character Buddy in the movie *Wall Street*, convinced that greed is good—and yet not convinced at all.

Finally, one day when I was about to head out of town with my cousins to Martha's Vineyard, Karen pushed me to the breaking point. She arrived at the office with packed bags. "Where are you going?" I asked her in the reception area, though I had an awful feeling I already knew.

"It's none of your business. I'm free to go wherever I like," she replied equably. Then she admitted that she was also going to Martha's Vineyard. "I'd like to get to know your cousins better. After all, Jim is a client of ours." I felt rage build up in me like steam percolating out of a geothermal geyser. It was impossible to avoid an eruption.

"I've had it," I yelled. "I quit."

She paled and backed away from me. "What do you mean?"

"I no longer work here." My heart beat rapidly, but I felt tremendous relief.

"You'll regret it," she said darkly. "You'll see."

I gave two weeks' notice and for most of those two weeks worked from my home. On my last day as an employee of Z Development, I celebrated by staying in bed all day.

After many nights of poor sleep, an idea popped into my head: I would take up photography again. My soul craved creativity; I needed to do something that felt positive and concrete. I began thinking back to the days I'd spent in Chinatown in 1980, camera in hand. As I strolled the streets, I saw life—a life I didn't have. My subjects then were Chinese elderly, children playing and men gambling in the parks, and homeless men sleeping on benches or begging for money.

One morning in January 1990 I went down to Penn Camera Exchange, the best camera store in D.C., and bought a new Nikon with a portrait lens. That afternoon I enrolled in a photography course at the Corcoran School of Art, which gave me access to a complete dark room. The smell of the chemicals brought memories of joy—something I needed to wash me clean of my associations with Karen. I would go out the next Saturday and shoot some new images.

The morning arrived, cold and bracing. Deciding not to shower or shave, I noticed as I brushed my teeth that the bags under my eyes from a week of poor sleep helped with the look I was going for. I dressed in my worst jeans, a black turtleneck, and, for warmth, an old, ripped ski parka. I took out my camera, covered its logo with blue duct tape, and grabbed six rolls of black-and-white film from the refrigerator. I emptied my wallet of most of its cash and all credit cards. Then I was outside, striding in the crisp morning air toward downtown D.C., my camera slung from my shoulder.

I walked down 18th Street looking for homeless people. I took a few side streets, then edged near the underside of the Rock Creek Park Highway, where a few days earlier I'd seen a camp of street people sheltering from the rain. Cautiously, I moved closer.

A man and a woman sat on a couch under the overpass. The woman's dirty brown hair had matted into a sort of net around her head. The right side of her face was bandaged in gauze, a black eye shining above the dressing. Several of her teeth were missing. She took a swig from a large bottle of rum and handed it to the large black man next to her. He was tall with an Abe Lincoln beard, a black ski hat pulled down close to his eyes, which were clear despite the alcohol. He looked strong and fit, as if he'd played football in his youth—not the type of person one wanted to mess with. He was talking to an older, short guy with wavy gray hair who sat perched on a refrigerator turned on its side. His jeans were stained with oil, and despite the cold he wore only a short-sleeved shirt. A large tattoo adorned his forearm; it was a figure of a woman and, underneath, "Lisa."

"If you take a picture, I'll break your camera," the big guy growled when he saw me. He got up from the couch and moved toward me.

For a second I thought how nice it would be to be back in my apartment, with the heat on and a new video playing on the VCR. I took a step backward. "Okay, I won't," I said, putting the lens cap back on the camera and shifting it behind my back. He went back to the couch.

"Do you mind if I join you?" I asked hesitantly.

"Suit yourself, but no pictures," the woman said. I walked over to an old beat-up chair and sat down.

"What are you doing with that camera?" the woman asked. "You aren't with the press, are you?"

"No. I'm a photography student," I said. "I'm working on a class project."

"That's cool," the woman said. They passed around the rum again, and offered me a hit. I accepted, surprising myself.

"It's all right if you want to take our picture," the big guy said after we'd sat together about thirty minutes, talking some, sitting with our own thoughts some. "We don't mind."

I took several shots of each of them, getting much closer than I had in my earlier street portrait work at Stanford. Back then, I was too removed from my subjects, afraid to make their acquaintance. With these shots, however, the rapport I'd established could be seen in the finished photos. My new friends' eyes were warm and shining rather than glazed and distant.

As I walked home, I felt the two rolls of film in my pocket and was happy for the first time in months. I'd forgotten how great it felt to have a camera in my hands. It was pure. You see it, you shoot it, you develop and print it.

Although I was rusty at the beginning of my course at the Corcoran, after a month, the shooting and darkroom skills came back to me. I loved the hours spent in the dark sloshing chemicals around, watching my subjects come to life. Unleashing my creative spirit jump-started my soul, which had felt dead.

A few months later, I was proud to display my street portraits along with a short narrative in the Corcoran's student show. I called them "Reflections from the Street."

CHAPTER 5

The Seeds of Green

I WENT BACK TO WORK for my cousins, who happily took me back, even suggesting that if I played my cards right I would become president of the construction firm. I worked for Jim this time, learning to estimate construction plans and write bids. I was in the area of tenant improvements: building out the interior space for offices and a few retail tenants. Although Jim's staff treated me as a member of the team, I will never forget the heavy feeling of being a project manager with a beeper on my belt. Every time it vibrated, an owner was calling to tell me about something that had gone wrong.

Diane and Jim could see that I had little enthusiasm for my work. One day in 1991 they gave me a new assignment. "Why don't you use your business acumen to diversify the company?" Diane said to me over dinner at Duke Ziebert's Restaurant on Connecticut Avenue. "The market is terrible and we need to find other areas to leverage our core strengths." Jim, who was eating the famous crab cakes, nodded in agreement. I was swept with a sense of relief. For the first time in months I didn't feel pressure in my chest.

I floundered around for a few months, unsure what direction we should take. Then one day I learned about a new project we

were building out for the Washington office of the Environmental
Defense Fund. The project manager for Jim's firm didn't know
what to make of "environmental" design. The next day I toured
the space, which had been designed by a young New York architect named William McDonough. EDF's space had been
designed with energy-efficient lighting fixtures that bounced most
of the light off the ceiling, paint that had omitted the toxic preser-
vatives, natural linoleum floor tiles, bathroom ceramic tiles made
from recycled glass, and partitions made from recycled plastic bottles. It was an amazing eye-opener. No one in our office had ever
heard either of McDonough or of sustainable design. Some of the
principles of energy efficiency and waste recycling were known,
but the concepts of sustainable materials and indoor air quality
were brand new. Focusing on energy and resource efficiency and
occupant health made sense to me—it tied into the ethics that
Professor Masters had drilled into us at Stanford—but I'd never
thought of it in such a holistic way before.

As a developer, I often encountered quite a different scenario
from what McDonough was attempting to do. Not long before
this, I'd gone with Jim to a demolition site at 12th and Pennsylvania, at the old Post building. Part of the structure was being
saved, to be integrated into a new building that Jim's company
was in charge of constructing. The rest was being junked.
Overhead, a huge crane swung a massive concrete wrecking ball
at the building. As the big ball bashed into the building, debris
crashed down—pieces of glass, concrete, brick, steel framing, and
drywall. Dust coated my shoes. "What are they going to do with
all of that?" I shouted at Jim.

"Take it to the dump." Jim waved his hand at trucks waiting in
a line to cart off the waste.

"Why didn't they try to save the whole building?" I yelled. It looked perfectly good to me: beautiful details on the façade, the masonry work of a high quality, no doubt done by real craftsmen in the early 1900s.

"It'd cost too much money to renovate," Jim said over the noise. "It's a good thing the building wasn't historic, or the cost would be 50 percent higher. Getting the approvals would have added another year to the schedule."

"Why aren't they recycling the building elements?" I asked. The recycling movement nationwide was gaining momentum; people everywhere were now recycling glass, newspaper, and plastic bottles.

"No one does that. Takes too much time—makes the job cost more. Besides, no one wants that junk," he said, motioning at the pile of debris, now about twenty feet high.

We left the site and went over to an enormous, newly built office building at 18th and Pennsylvania. The several-hundred-thousand-square-foot, twelve-story building was for a high-technology company due to move in within two weeks, and Jim's firm was scrambling to finish the interior.

The top floor was pandemonium, with workers swarming everywhere. The walls were up and being painted. Carpet was being glued down in the hallway. The air reeked of chemicals. I sneezed repeatedly and my eyes teared as I inhaled the fumes. Looking around, I noticed the building didn't have operable windows. I wondered if they'd get the noxious smell out before the tenants moved in.

Even though daylight was streaming in on the south side of the building, the lights were on. "Jim, have you ever installed daylight dimmers in the overhead lights?" I'd read about them in a newsletter from PEPCO, the local utility.

"No. They're expensive, and I'm not sure they work," he shrugged.

And so it went. As landlords, we focused on designing attractive buildings and tenant spaces. We shopped in Italy for the marble for the façades and lobbies. Our architects worked hard to maximize the number of corner offices for big-shot lawyers, the prime tenants in our buildings. We didn't worry about energy efficiency because we passed the expense of operating the buildings on to the tenants.

With all this in my head—the waste at the construction site, sealed windows and toxic carpets at the new offices, and what McDonough had done in the EDF space—I began studying ways to incorporate environmentally friendly elements into building and office design.

A system rating buildings for green elements had been developed in England, and another one was being created in Canada. There was nothing at all similar in the United States. To gather information, I went over to the Department of Energy and also visited several divisions of the U.S. Environmental Protection Agency. The focus of both these agencies was mostly on energy efficiency and waste reduction, though the EPA had recently set up an indoor air quality division. I was flipping through architectural magazines at the office, researching building materials that had low emission levels of volatile organic compounds (VOCs), when I saw an announcement for a meeting of the newly formed Committee of the Environment at the American Institute of Architects' national headquarters at 17th and New York Avenue.

The next week, I went to the meeting. The AIA is lodged in a six-story semicircular concrete building; it shares a huge courtyard with the Octagon Museum, which fronts the street. I found the meeting room and took a seat in the back; as a nonmember, I didn't want to draw attention to myself. The committee had formed about a year before under the leadership of an architect from Kansas City named Bob Berkebile, and he was the one who opened the meeting. About thirty architects then proceeded to speak over each other, interrupting and shouting things out, as they discussed a book they were producing, with funding from the EPA, called the *Environmental Resource Guide*. Two chapters were being added, calculating the environmental impacts of a product from beginning to the end of its life. The calculation started with the extraction energy and environmental impact of the various raw materials that went into fabrication, and continued through the input of additional resource flows and ecological ramifications of the manufacturing process, construction, and ongoing use. This full systems approach appealed to my engineering background.

The committee was sponsoring several lectures on sustainable building at the upcoming national AIA convention in Boston. As I've already explained, I went to that 1992 convention, and those three days changed my life.

On the airplane back to D.C. from Boston I replayed in my mind all that I'd learned at the meeting. Putting my hand to my head, I could almost feel it pulsating. I felt as if I'd witnessed the start of a revolution in how we make buildings. The speakers had explained the elements of the new discipline, but it hadn't yet taken root in the industry, and the fundamentals weren't established. Even the definition of sustainable building wasn't clear. Only a handful of projects in the entire country had been designed in an ecological way. Europe was more advanced, but only by a few years. Forms of renewable energy, such as solar and

fuel cells, were still in their infancy—and in that realm, NASA
had done much of the pioneering work.

I'd asked manufacturers' representatives staffing vendor booths
at the conference if they had any environmental products. They
looked at me as if I'd been smoking dope. "All of our products are
environmentally sensitive," one said to me. "We meet all of the
building codes and ASTM fireproof standards." (I later learned
that ASTM—the American Society of Testing and Materials—sets
many of the country's product standards.)

Now, as I sat staring at the patchwork of farms below the plane,
I again let the excitement wash over me. At last I had found my
lifework.

The next week I dragged Diane and Jim to Manhattan to meet
Bill McDonough. His long hair was slicked back, and he wore the
same bow tie he'd worn in Boston. He spoke with the unmistak-
able inflections of New England. We were looking at a photo of a
high-rise that looked like a modern leaning tower of Pisa, only it
wasn't leaning. "This is a building I designed for a competition in
Poland," he said. "And this"—he produced another photo, of a
small wood house with a sloping roof covered with solar panels—
"is a solar home I built while I was an architecture student at Yale.
It was my first sustainable project."

Diane shifted in her seat and looked at her watch. Jim gazed at
the framed photos of buildings on the wall. Bill pulled some more
renderings and photos from his portfolio.

"How many of your projects actually got built, besides the solar
house?" Jim asked. I tensed. Diane doodled on her pad.

"The Poland project was just a design concept. It never got
built, but all of the homes did," Bill said. "I'm also working on a
sustainable modular home concept for Russia."

Jim perked up. "We're doing some work in Russia"—his New York accent seemed to become more pronounced—"supervising the design and construction of over a thousand homes. And Ariel Sharon has also asked us to do some work in Israel."

"That's fascinating," Bill said politely. He leaned forward. "I'm raising capital for our modular project. Should I send you some information?"

Jim sat back, tapping a pencil, and looked at Diane. She studied her doodle, an intricate geometric pattern running down the left margin of the notepad. "Sure," he said. I felt a movement, and was pretty sure it was Diane kicking Jim under the table.

"Well, this has been interesting," Diane said. She looked at her watch again. "We have another appointment." The meeting was over.

That afternoon we met with Randy Croxton, the sustainable architect for a National Audubon renovation project I'd first heard about at the AIA convention in Boston. Before starting his own firm, Croxton had worked with I.M. Pei Architects, an internationally renowned firm. He was also the architect for the Natural Resources Defense Council's New York office. Completed in 1989, it was the first sustainably designed space in the country, addressing light, air, energy, and occupant health and productivity.

I had visited the NRDC offices on West Twentieth Street the day before. The quality of the daylighting immediately struck me. Although it was cloudy outside, the space was bright—enough to read in comfortably. Windows lined the perimeter while skylights allowed light in from above. Croxton had also installed sensors that controlled the overhead lights with electronic ballasts; they turned on only if the daylight fell below a certain level. I'd learned that the lighting system was 75 percent more efficient than the norm. The carpet was made from recycled coke bottles. It looked and felt like Astroturf.

The idea in these early experiments in green building was to reduce the amount of waste. I'd learned at the Boston conference that construction contributed 20 percent of the waste choking our landfills. Over the past decade communities within the United States had established recycling programs, but the number of products—especially building products—made from recycled material was still low. The NRDC and the Audubon projects had recycled a good portion of their construction and demolition debris. Many materials, such as old carpeting and lighting fixtures, were salvaged and reused, while items such as concrete and wood were recycled. All paints, adhesives, and glued wood products were made with low-toxicity materials. In the NRDC space, Croxton had installed a series of air filters and efficient HVAC equipment. The level of fresh air supplied to the space was six times higher than required by the prevailing standard; it even provided a slight breeze.

I had told Diane about Croxton's innovations, but she remained unconvinced, even after our New York meetings. "I'm not sure how much of this field is just smoke and mirrors versus real science," she said. "But let's continue to explore."

Over the next two months I conducted research as if I were looking for buried gold. I continued to go to the AIA Committee of the Environment's meetings—usually the only nonarchitect in attendance. Otherwise, I worked the phone like a graduate student researching for his dissertation, and when materials arrived, I would read and read. Heaped on my night table at home, the floor around my bed, and my dresser were all manner of environmental books. However, I found little literature on sustainable building. The best up-to-date source was the Worldwatch Institute, the producer of the annual industry bible, *State of the World*, their annual environmental trends report, *Vital Signs*, and dozens of white papers. These documents armed me with statistics on the ecological damage our postindustrial society was wreaking on the planet. Though depressing, this information about our shrinking natural resources and increasing pollution encouraged me in my quest. The building industry, I learned, was a place where a person could make a real difference.

At work I pored through manufacturers' catalogs, looking for sustainable products. I became friends with people at the Department of Energy's Office of Building Technology and EPA's Indoor Air Quality Division and Green Lights program. Green Lights urged energy efficiency in lighting; it was assisted in this effort by PEPCO, the local utility, which offered cash rebates for installation of more efficient lighting fixtures, electronic ballasts, and mechanical system motors. As a result of such measures, the voluntary participants in the Green Lights program found their electricity bills reduced by as much as 50 percent. I also visited PEPCO to find out what they were doing to encourage sustainability.

Learning about individual governmental programs was a challenge. Each agency, and even divisions within a given agency, operated independently. At one point, I realized that I'd visited a dozen different agencies and divisions—probably the only person ever to do this. I thought of publishing a directory for my new friends at the AIA.

One day I trekked out to suburban Maryland to tour a house made of recycled-content materials. It was a hot day, and the house smelled a bit like the landfill it was made of. Even though it performed well as an example of waste diversion, the designers hadn't understood the greater importance of indoor air quality and hence occupant health.

The word *green* began to pop up as an alternative to *sustainable*. To me it had a broader connotation, incorporating the economic advantages of an efficient and healthy building.

I learned that an environmental building could reduce annual energy and water costs, not to mention landfill and transport fees for dumping construction debris. Improved indoor air quality meant workers would get sick less—an enormous financial advantage for any company. These were arguments that would impress Diane and other building owners, I hoped.

I bought a forest green suit to symbolize my new creed. I also became obsessed with recycling at home, ferrying my bottles, cans, and newspapers to a local drop-off point every week without fail. I even set up a recycling system for Diane and Jim's house—while trying not to think about the five heat pumps needed to cool their home during the sweltering summers. "There goes Mr. Green," coworkers would say to me as I walked down the hallway at work.

Wanting to understand environmental laws and standards better, I asked around and was referred to Mike Italiano, an environmental partner in a three-hundred-lawyer D.C. law firm called Bell, Boyd, and Lloyd. Mike also chaired the Environmental Assessment and Risk Management Committee at ASTM.

When I met Mike at his firm's fancy offices at Sixteenth and L Streets, I liked him immediately. He looked to be in his mid-forties, with an athletic build and classic Italian looks: slicked-back jet-black hair, a bushy mustache, alert dark-brown eyes, and olive skin. His stride was so fast that he swept rather than led me to his office from the reception area. And his office demonstrated his vigorous energy: client files everywhere, regulatory books in piles on the floor, telephone messages scattered over the desk.

"We're thinking of getting into the environmental business in a way that complements our construction company," I said. Mike pulled out a legal pad and entered the date and starting time of our conference. As I spoke, he scribbled words that to me were illegible.

"I've seen your signs," Mike said. If you lived or worked in D.C., it was hard to miss Jim's signs: They were on dozens of buildings and hundred-foot construction cranes throughout the city, our firm name and logo boldly displayed in yellow letters on a bright-blue background. The signs were lit so they could be seen even at night. I often kidded Jim that he charged lower fees if the signage potential was great. He never took one down unless the owner called to complain.

As we launched into our meeting, Mike told me about ASTM and his environmental committee. I learned that ASTM was founded about a hundred years ago. Its thirty thousand voluntary members develop thousands of standards for materials, products, systems, and services. ASTM standards for building products were cited in building codes, governmental regulations, and laws, as well as specified by architects in their building plans.

Under Mike's leadership, the Environmental Assessment and Risk Management Committee started in 1990 and now boasted about a thousand members. It created a standard that was one of ASTM's most successful, coming up with an efficient and cheap way for developers of commercial real estate to check a site for contaminants. When I was a developer, an environmental site assessment cost about $25,000. After Mike's committee's standard was approved, the cost dropped below $1,000.

Mike's specialty was environmental litigation, mostly Superfund work. He'd written a book on leaky underground fuel tanks. He advised manufacturers on product development and defense against liability, and had done some work with building owners.

Mike's depth of knowledge and enthusiasm were impressive—and infectious. "I can help you survey the environmental build-ing industry options and formulate a business plan," he said as we shook hands goodbye. "If you're interested, I can pull together a panel of experts to help brainstorm. I'd also like to get you involved in ASTM."

Diane let me hire Mike to conduct the brainstorm and write a summary report. It was the start of a long-term alliance and, more important, made me feel less alone in my new passion. Mike worked with me as if I was his partner or brother, not just a client.

"David, you need to stop doing research and figure something out," Diane said to me one day over salads at Houston's restaurant on lower Wisconsin Avenue. "This is costing us a lot of money." I suddenly lost my appetite. I'd been worried that this was coming, but was so enthralled with the research and networking that I'd delayed figuring out the question my employers were paying me to answer: How we could make money.

For the next week I holed up in my office, taking lunch at my desk. Diane came several times a day to see what I was up to, but I wouldn't show her anything until I'd finished. I was hatching a plan for a sustainable building firm to be a subsidiary of Jim's con-struction company. The new firm would provide consulting ser-vices to organizations wanting a "green building" or office suite, with Jim's firm getting the contracts to do the work.

After Mike Italiano reviewed the plan for me, I printed it on green paper and, with my heart in my mouth, submitted it to our management team. We scheduled a meeting for the following week to discuss it.

. As the week crawled by I grew increasingly nervous. The morning of the meeting I'd been unable to eat my bran cereal or drink any coffee. When we assembled in the small glass conference room—I was wearing my green suit and a tie decorated with bright yellow flowers—everyone had my green document in front of them. I kept looking from one face to the other, trying to read their expressions. If they didn't like my plan, I'd have to go back to construction.

"Good plan," Diane said at once.

"I like it, too," Jim said. "What's the first step in setting up the new company?" Relief flooded through me. I reached for a bagel and started outlining my ideas.

Over the next few months we formed Katz Environmental Consulting, complete with new logo, letterhead (printed on recycled paper with soy inks), and a brochure describing our services. I set up a sustainable products library to use once I landed our first project. My title was Managing Director.

At that time—1992—there were just a few other green building consulting firms in the country: Rocky Mountain Institute's Green Development Services, headed up by Bill Browning; and E2 in Los Angeles, run by John Picard. Picard and I met on one of my trips home to visit my parents; he'd just started working with Southern California Gas Company on a green renovation project in Downey called the Energy Resource Center.

A couple of weeks after our brochures arrived, Diane began to push me. Over take-out soup and salads in her office she said, "Get out there, David, and find us some clients. This is a business." She pointed her spoon at me.

I *had* been dragging my feet, not sure how to sell our new services. I'd never faced making cold calls before. The next day I got a directory of environmental organizations and started to gain momentum. However, the term "green building" was not known and when I tried to explain it to potential clients, they lost interest.

Mike Italiano assured me that I'd find the business. One night I joined him and four of his ASTM colleagues for drinks at the Marriott on Pennsylvania Avenue. They'd worked together for many years, and the bantering made them seem more like family than business associates. I saw a jovial and playful side to Mike that reminded me of my older brothers. I later learned he was the eldest of three boys.

"Hey, David," Mike said during a lull in the conversation. "How would you like to become chair of a new ASTM subcommittee on green building?" I flushed—in part because I was flattered, and even more because I was terrified.

"I don't know anything about ASTM or the standard setting process," I protested.

"We consider that a plus," Mike said. "Don't worry, we'll back you up. The next meeting is in Philadelphia. Why don't you join us? It'll be fun."

I told him so little had been written on drafting standards for green building that I had no idea where to start. "Just invent it," he said easily. "It's better to define it yourself than wait for the market. Speed is quality."

I must have looked doubtful. "Tell Diane that this will put your company on the map," Mike urged. "Being chair of an ASTM subcommittee is a big deal."

Diane agreed, and within a month I'd formed my group, with Bill Browning as vice chair. After several animated meetings, our green building subcommittee membership grew to well over a hundred, but we still had no product. I finally holed myself up for an entire weekend and wrote the first draft of an attempt to define a green building standard and its practices, covering areas like energy, water and resource efficiency, indoor environmental quality, and waste minimization. The draft even went on to outline ways to carry out green construction and building operations.

When I printed out the document, it was fifty pages long. "Wow," I thought as I flipped through it, "where did all these ideas come from?"

We sent the draft standard to our subcommittee for comments and, after revision, to Mike's full committee via a letter ballot. This is a formal procedure in which committee members have the opportunity to comment on the draft. All negative comments must be addressed—either by resolving them or by voting them as nonpersuasive. To my chagrin, we received dozens of negatives, and after an entire day of working on the revisions we still hadn't addressed all of them. Smoking became a big item of discussion. Three members tried to convince me that smoking was acceptable in buildings if a room was provided with separately ducted ventilation. Even though this solution was preferable to allowing unrestricted smoking inside, I fought the idea like a trapped tiger. From an investigative article in the *Washington Post*, I later learned that the smoking supporters were funded by the Tobacco Institute. They had unlimited funds to fight me, as did some of the large product manufacturers who wanted to slow us down, fearing that the standard would hurt their business. Another complaint came from a member from a major manufacturing firm who said that the information I'd written was "anecdotal" and needed hard statistics. I agreed, but the data that he wanted simply didn't exist.

Mike had told me that the ASTM consensus process was powerful, but it sure was laborious. I'd never been an especially patient sort, and the process began to wear me down. I understood that ASTM standards were important, becoming part of the building code and even law, but I found it frustrating that a single dissenter with ample funds and time could put things on hold virtually forever.

I did enjoy one aspect of the ASTM work immensely, however, and that was the core group of passionate people I'd assembled in our green building subcommittee. They represented all sectors of the industry: building owners, manufacturers, environmental consulting firms, insurance companies, government, architects, engineers, and contractors. The talks we had at meetings, and afterward over drinks and a meal, positively sizzled. Although we didn't know it at the time, we were inventing a new way of approaching the design, construction, and operation of buildings. By looking at the building holistically, as a collective of individual disciplines, we could identify and lend strength to the interconnected areas.

Take energy efficiency, for example. Traditionally, this area belonged to the building engineers, who chose energy-efficient equipment and control systems to heat and cool the interior space so that occupants are comfortable whether it's snowing outside or one hundred degrees and humid. But, as I learned, if you want to minimize a building's energy use, you must start with its architecture, not with its mechanical systems. The architect and planner need to first fine-tune the building's siting on the property, its massing and footprint, the shading potential, wall and roof insulation, glazing performance, roof color, and daylight penetration. All of these factors change the design requirements and the building's energy systems.

Another example: The engineers typically viewed indoor air quality as a ventilation strategy, relying on the mechanical system to exhaust and then filter polluted indoor air before reintroducing it as recirculated air. I learned from my new green architect friends that to provide for the highest level of indoor air quality, we first need to select and install building products that don't off-gas volatile organic compounds. Selecting alternative, nontoxic cleaning products is also critical. In addition, in those instances where the outside air quality is poor—such as a location next to a freeway—a higher level of filtration will be required. The same is true for recirculated air within the building.

We began to ask manufacturers for more information about their products, like the off-gassing profile over time as shown in an air chamber test. Our concern about the environmental performance of building products and systems was entirely new, and although a few of the more progressive manufacturers understood the importance of providing these data, the majority resisted. In many cases, the company didn't have access to the information itself, and the cost of obtaining it could add up to hundreds of thousands of dollars. But we were asking the questions—and that's how change begins.

Meanwhile, I'd managed to interest a few companies—clients of Jim's—in finding out more about energy efficiency services. Calculating the return on investment for energy-efficient measures is easier than trying to sell a complete sustainable-building approach, so we started there: at the pocketbook. Each month these clients receive a utility bill. We suggested to them that if we made their lights and heating system more efficient, and the bill dropped 30 percent, they'd be better off.

Return on investment is easy to calculate when it comes to utility costs; it is more difficult in other areas, such as improved indoor air quality and recycled-content materials. Yet my heart was set on delivering a full green building menu. Seeing the projects that had been carried out for the Audubon Society, Natural Resources Defense Council, and Environmental Defense Fund convinced me that our best bet was nonprofit and environmental organizations. And Washington was the national headquarters for such groups.

Having narrowed my target audience, each morning I sent out introductory letters with our brochure of services to a dozen organizations, linking their specific mission to the environmental quality and performance of their office space. Finally, one took the bait: Greenpeace. To my disappointment, however, our meeting revealed that although there was interest, they were in the middle of a ten-year lease and not sure of their future office space plans.

Jim's firm, meanwhile, was bidding on the build-out of new offices for a branch of Blue Cross. We submitted two bids: one for the standard plans and specifications as designed, and my alternate environmental bid. I was distressed when they didn't even respond. Jim's bid was high and he lost as well.

Still, specifying and sourcing out alternative green products was good practice for me. The products I'd entered in my bid included environmental carpets, adhesives, paint, ceiling tile, and ceramic tile with recycled content, lower emissions of VOCs, and energy efficiency lighting systems with sensors (including both occupancy controls and daylight dimmers). Unfortunately, at that time, because of low demand they cost more. I hoped that ecological- and health-oriented organizations would pay more for the chance to have their buildings reflect their principles. As the Blue Cross bid proved, that wasn't necessarily going to be the case. "This all remains to be seen," Diane told me with pursed lips after we lost that bid. "You may be wearing rose-colored glasses."

The turning point came when we bid a tenant improvement project for Worldwatch Institute. One day, while flipping through their latest edition of *State of the World*, I saw that they were located nearby on Massachusetts Avenue. I called them up and, amazingly enough, learned that they were about to renovate their offices. I scheduled a meeting with their chief administrative officer, Claudine.

A few days later, again dressed in my green suit with flowered tie, I drove to the office of Worldwatch, arriving ten minutes early. The walls were decorated with framed covers of their many books, including *State of the World* and *Vital Signs*. There were also photos of the earth and many of animals and nature scenes. I looked up at the lights—they were inefficient fluorescents, and the wall sconces had incandescent bulbs (which consume energy to provide 10 percent light versus 90 percent heat). The air smelled stale. I looked down at the carpet and saw that it was old, then glanced over at the windows: They were inoperable.

I watched as Claudine walked into the reception area. She held herself straight, and her dress was D.C. conservative: long blue skirt, white blouse, and yellow scarf. I'd expected an outfit more Berkeley style: blue jeans and something flowery on top, with enormous hoop earrings. She extended her hand and we shook stiffly, then she led me into a small conference room, its bookshelves packed with environmental books. I hoped I could spend some time looking at the titles.

"I've got a meeting in about twenty minutes," Claudine said, looking at her watch. "Tell me what you've got." I took a deep breath. This was my chance.

"I run the environmental division of Katz Construction," I said, trying to sound confident. I gave her my most winning smile and leaned forward. "I know that your new office space is already designed, but if you add us to your bidders list, I'll figure out how to green it. We specify energy-efficient lighting systems, water-efficient fixtures for the bathroom, and healthy and resource-efficient building materials: carpeting, paint, cabinet substrate, ceiling tile. I will also calculate the PEPCO rebate you'll get for the energy-efficient items."

"We're on a tight budget," she said, chewing on her pen. My head started to pound.

"A green approach does cost more, but the rebate helps," I assured her. "The market for green products is just starting. It takes environmental organizations like yours to jump-start it. Your books speak to the enormous environmental impact of our buildings and the products we manufacture. Designing a green space would be an example to the public." I paused. She shifted in her seat, and my stomach lurched. "We could even do a white paper on the environmental benefits," I went on hurriedly. "It would be a great case study. The only other green space I know of in D.C. is the one we just built out for the Environmental Defense Fund." She looked at her watch. "I'd be pleased to give you a tour," I added hopelessly.

"We *have* published extensively on energy efficiency, but as I said, we have limited funds." Claudine began to shuffle he. papers.

I exhaled in exasperation. "Look, I'll add you to the bidders list." She stood up, indicating that the session was over.

I walked back to my car in a daze. She'd showed little interest in our environmental services. I had thought she'd congratulate me or something, but no, it was all about the money. Could she have misunderstood? I stopped walking, realizing I'd gone right past my car.

The next week I worked around the clock developing two bids for Worldwatch: one for the plans and specifications as designed (non-green), and the other, our recommended green upgrade. The green bid was 10 percent higher, though the rebate brought it down two points. I hoped they would see that paying an extra 8 percent was worth it.

I didn't hear anything over the following week. When Claudine didn't return my call, I phoned her construction manager. "We awarded the bid to another firm. You weren't the low bidder," he said.

"What about our environmental bid?" I asked.

"That was even higher than your base bid. Sorry."

I hung up the phone, missing the cradle. My legs felt heavy when I rose to go tell Diane the news. If Worldwatch wouldn't pay to green their building, who would?

"I can't believe that we lost," Diane said. "They didn't even respond?" I remained silent as she shook her head in dismay.

I went back to my office and picked up *State of the World* and threw it in the trash, then headed for the door. A few minutes later I was in the car, driving home. I slammed the door of my loft apartment behind me and double-locked it. My apartment felt foreign, as if I'd walked into someone else's home. When had I bought all that stuff? The black leather couch and sofa chair, Italian glass dining room table with its high-tech chairs, enormous Sony TV and component stereo. When had I started to need a $1,500 signature glass table to hold my mail? Glancing at the huge colorful ceramic bowl that Diane and Jim had given me for my birthday, I kicked off my Kenneth Cole shoes so hard that one slammed into the wall. I looked down at my clothes: a Hugo

Boss suit and matching tailored shirt that together had cost over $1,000; an Hermès tie I'd bought in Paris. On my wrist was the Cartier watch Diane and Jim had given me. It felt as if it was cutting off my circulation.

I changed into an old pair of jeans and a fly-fishing T-shirt from a trip I'd taken with my father and brothers several summers ago in Montana. My movements were jerky, my breathing ragged. I pulled out one of my favorite movies, *Mr. Holland's Opus*, and put it into the VCR. Seeing the difference Mr. Holland makes in the lives of thousands of students as their teacher and mentor had always warmed my soul. As it began to play, I took out the pint of Ben and Jerry's Chunky Monkey that I'd bought on the way home and shoveled the ice cream into my mouth. Although it didn't fit my health-conscious diet at all, for the amount of time it took to eat the million calories and large chocolate chunks, I felt calmer. Whoever invented the flavor must have felt pissed off like this too.

I tried to concentrate on the movie. Mr. Holland was teaching his class about rock and roll—a breakthrough in his once-boring teaching style. He'd figured out how to reach them. To the right of the TV I saw the photo of an old girlfriend, Lauren. We'd gone out for about three months, but it didn't work out. "You're too picky," my mother had told me when I broke up with her. "Unless you ease up, you'll be alone your whole life."

"I told you to go talk to the rabbi for names of single women," my dad added to the conversation. But how could a rabbi know who was right for me?

The phone rang, but I didn't answer. I wiped the sweat off my forehead. It was August and humid. What did I have to show for my decade here? I still owned the Arlington building with my partners, but Control Data had moved out and we were losing

$30,000 a month. I went to get a glass of water from the kitchen. The door of the closet in the living room was ajar. My eye fell on my blue suitcase.

"Do not confuse effort with results," my father had said a hundred times, and that phrase came back to me as I began throwing my clothes into the bag. To him, money was one of the key measurements of success. But he had also quoted Shakespeare's advice to Polonius when he'd sent me off to Stanford, "To thine own self be true." The more I solely pursued monetary success, the less I was able to breathe. Another voice was welling up inside me. With my whole being, I yearned for something different. But what?

Part Two: Green

CHAPTER 6

Down and Out in San Francisco

"WAKE UP, SACK, it's morning," my college buddy, Jeff Davis, said. It was October 1992, 5:30 A.M. and still dark outside in San Francisco's foggy Marina district. I was lying on Jeff's apartment floor, which was cold, but the sagging couch hurt my back. I pulled the blue sleeping bag over my head and shut my eyes. Jeff kicked me. I squinted up at his beaming face—his teeth were annoyingly white. My legs felt heavy and achy, my back, tight from sleeping on the floor, my head, thick with sleep.

Jeff prodded me again and clapped his hands in my face. "Come on, we're going to the gym." He wore black lycra pants, T-shirt, and running shoes. Jeff was always training for a triathlon. On my last visit he'd taken me on what he called a "short bike ride." After five hours and three major hills, sweat streamed down my face and my historically fragile back was in spasm. I wanted to get off and walk, or even lie down, but thought it better to endure the pain than admit my weakness. Jeff himself had hardly broken a sweat. "Isn't this fun?" he bubbled.

I'd met Jeff when we were both freshmen at Stanford. We'd joined the same fraternity, SAE, although I quickly became convinced I'd never fit into the house. The nadir was Hell Week, when each of us was assigned some sophomoric task—letting a mouse go at a McDonald's at Fisherman's Wharf, painting UC

79

Berkeley's big white C on the hill Stanford red, driving a golf cart nude through the library's first floor. Jeff's task was to drive in reverse through the tollbooth on the Bay Bridge. We thought this was hysterical, until the police gave him a $250 ticket. My assignment was to get on a United Airlines plane bound for Hawaii and nab a *Hemispheres* magazine—all without a ticket or getting arrested. I tried telling them my grandmother was on board and had forgotten her mink coat. I even had a mink coat that Cliff, my big brother at SAE, had lent me. When this aroused a security agent's suspicion, I leveled with him, and he got me a copy of the magazine.

Jeff and I were both engineers who loved photography, travel, and philosophizing about life. Our fathers both ran their own businesses and wanted us to follow their paths. When Jeff's dad's company went public in the mid '80s, my dad and I bought some stock, and later sold it at a profit.

"Can you help me prepare for the accounting exam?" Jeff asked me during our first quarter in the fraternity. We had several classes together. Always prepared, I explained the material to him. He got 100. I got 92.

After Stanford he worked at IBM and, like many of our classmates, got a Harvard MBA. After a stint as general manager of Lucas Film's THX division, he cofounded a software production company called Lumen. When I arrived that October he and his partner, Glenn, were still in the start-up stage, inventing products for kindergarten through the twelfth grade that merged the fun of games with learning.

I couldn't sleep while being kicked, so I let Jeff drag me along to the Bay Club, a fancy multilevel gym on Battery Street with state-of-the-art equipment, a basketball court, and a large swimming pool. Jeff pushed me onto a bike, the stair machine, and into the cold pool. I swam a few laps, then huddled on a bench watching him do lap after lap with a fancy flip turn, his little red swim cap a blur in the water. I looked down at my belly. I was carrying an extra ten or twenty pounds. When did I get that? My mind wasn't on getting fit. I felt more like curling up in a ball and sleeping for a month.

"Have oatmeal and a bowl of fruit," Jeff chided me at the gym's health food bar afterward when I ordered a pastry and cup of strong coffee. I obeyed, then realized I felt better after the workout and healthy breakfast.

Jeff and I went to his office down Battery Street, four blocks from the gym. He had leased a large space with high ceilings, windows that opened, and lots of light. He and Glenn shared the suite with one other small business. When we entered, Led Zeppelin was playing on the stereo, and Glenn was bobbing his head in rhythm as he typed. Looking at his disheveled clothes, the same ones he'd worn the day before, I wondered if he actually lived in the office. "Jeff, you've gotta see this, dude," he exclaimed as we walked in. He showed us a new game and veered off into software jargon I couldn't understand, but Jeff nodded, obviously impressed.

Jeff then gave me a tour of the suite; he finished by saying, "Here's your office, David," and pointed at a small bright room overlooking the street. It had bare white walls and was sparsely furnished with a desk, chair, and phone. "Use it as long as you want. We'll deal with the rent when you figure out what you're going to do. I'm just happy to have someone uglier than me on the premises, sack-o." He patted me on the back and smiled.

Left alone, I sat down at the desk and, out of habit, pulled my Daytimer out of my briefcase. The month of October showed no appointments and no to-dos. I was thirty-two and unemployed. Most of my cash had evaporated when Control Data had moved and we'd found no replacement tenant. The night before, I'd had several nightmares. In one, I was in the back seat of Jim's car; he was driving, and Diane was putting on makeup next to him while lecturing me on my need to grow up. In another, I was in a meeting with my partners in the Arlington building, and they were all yelling at me. "You have a responsibility to stay here! You can't abandon the building!" one of them screamed.

After a while I went across the street to a small storefront selling fresh baked goods. The smell of coffee lured me in, and I bought a chocolate scone and a large coffee. The coffee was stronger and more bitter than any coffee I'd had in D.C., and the scone tasted pasty and weird. When I mentioned this to the cashier, she told me everything in the shop was organic, a word that didn't mean much to me at the time. Two guys at a table nearby were talking about a project deadline. "Do you think we can finish the graphics by Friday?" said a man whom I would have assumed was unemployed. He had on ripped blue jeans and sandals, and his T-shirt said, "Kill Your Television." In D.C. all the men wore a coat and tie, even at the height of summer's humidity and heat. Here in San Francisco, I felt like a square even wearing an oxford shirt and khakis—and people probably thought I was. I'd wear my David Bowie T-shirt tomorrow, I thought pathetically, feeling more sorry for myself than ever. I took my coffee to a nearby park and sat on a bench. Several homeless people slept on the grass under some trees; their tangled hair covered their faces. "Save some room for me, boys," I thought. On the way out of the park I threw my coffee cup into an overflowing trash can. It fell to the ground, so I picked it up and plodded around the block until I found an empty trash can. Then I took the long way back.

One afternoon I was sitting in my office in Jeff's suite, staring aimlessly at my framed black-and-white street photos from D.C. The one closest to me was of an old man sleeping on the sidewalk. He was bent in a fetal position, only one foot bearing a shoe. His coat was ripped at the shoulder and looked four sizes too big. He had a ski beanie on his head. His face was covered by an enormous gray beard, as if he hadn't shaved in a decade.

I fingered a hole in the knee of my jeans. This was the first time in my life when I wasn't sprinting toward a goal. All of my early schooling had been focused on my getting into a top college. My years at Stanford were intended to place me in an executive-level job or Ivy League grad school, and once the high-level job track came through, my D.C. years were dedicated to making money and starting my own business. Now I had no salary and a virtually nonexistent bank account. My lawyer had counseled me to settle a dispute that arose at the end of my D.C. days with the Columbia Pike building partners. Our main tenant, Control Data Learning Center, went out of business. Suddenly, we had a 50 percent vacant building and were losing $30,000 a month. I had one-third of the liability and couldn't afford to go too many rounds at that monthly loss. At the same time, I moved to California—upsetting my partners. I didn't want to go down with a sinking ship, so I hired a tough lawyer to negotiate an exit plan for me. "Take the deal" was his advice—the "deal" being that my father and I gave over our partnership interests, plus two cash payouts by me totaling around $100,000. I had just enough money to make the first one, and one year to figure out how to make the second one.

Asking my father to walk from his investment without compensation felt worse than losing one of my legs. Though he agreed to do it, I felt as if I'd blown my one shot to get him to invest in me.

Possibly not being able to include him in a venture ever again made me feel all the more alone.

I'd been aimlessly calling past acquaintances who worked with environmental and real estate development concerns, trying without much hope to see if I could generate a green consulting project. "I'll call you in a few weeks when I have more free time," the last guy I called had said, brushing me off.

"No problem. I understand." My head was throbbing as I hung up. I looked down at my desk. I'd scribbled about twenty names for a new green building consulting company on a legal pad. The only thing I could think to do was start my own firm, one similar to the one I'd started with my cousins. I hoped California, especially the Bay Area, was a better market than D.C. The best name on the list was ProTech—short for Progressive Technology Group. I'd already slashed a line through the others, and now I crossed out this last one too. It sounded too much like the noise made by a frog in the night.

"Forget the green; you'll starve. Why not go back to real estate development?" my father had said—a tape that played continually in my head. But I couldn't go back to work for a non-green company. Since leaving Washington I'd been unable to wear any of my suits, and was embarrassed to drive my BMW. The thought of working just for money seemed shallow. In fact, it made me nauseated.

I put the pad with the scratched-out names and a few papers into my briefcase. It was only three o'clock. I thought maybe I'd go back to Jeff's and take a nap or watch a video.

The phone rang. "Hey, David, it's Mike. How ya doing?" Mike Italiano was calling to check up on me. I'd reluctantly agreed to continue running the ASTM Green Building Subcommittee, but that volunteer effort was laborious and heavily political. What I needed was a job, not more volunteer work.

"When are you going to ballot your green building standard again?" Mike asked.

"We still need to beef up the document and collect more data," I told him, picking at the first pimple I'd had in eight years. "It's not ready yet." In fact, I had spent no time on the green building standard. I knew I was avoiding figuring out how, politically, to address the committee members who still advocated smoking in buildings. I felt like David against Goliath on that issue, except I was out of stones.

"The best way to get the additional information is to send it out to ballot. Our Phase One environmental site assessment standard was the fastest in ASTM history," Mike said in his brash East Coast manner. "Remember, speed is quality."

"Okay. I hear you," I said irritably. "I'll get on it. I was just heading out . . . "

"Not so fast," Mike said. "There's something else." I gritted my teeth; Mike could be heavy at times, staying on one topic until he was sure you understood his point. "I had lunch yesterday with an old law firm buddy of mine, Terry Bevels." Terry, it turned out, was a high-powered lobbyist with the Wexler Group, a full-service government affairs firm. His boss, Anne Wexler, had been a big shot in the Carter administration. Before that, Terry was with the Senate Appropriations Committee. "I told Terry about your ASTM subcommittee. He loves the idea of green buildings." I dropped my briefcase and sat. He had my attention now.

Mike said Terry had clients who wanted him to get money from Congress for new building projects. Terry's idea was to invent a demonstration green building program and include his clients' buildings in it.

"That sounds illegal," I said.

"It's done all the time," Mike assured me. "And Terry's the best." He paused. I opened my briefcase and pulled out my legal pad and a pen. I flipped past the crossed-out company names and turned to a new page. I would have dated the page at the top if I remembered the date.

"Okay, shoot," I said, sounding more enthusiastic now.

Mike said Terry wanted our help in creating the demonstration green building program. He mentioned several phases of congressional funding, the first one starting at $1 million for five projects. Two of the five projects were buildings for Terry's own clients: the New England Aquarium and the Lamont Doherty Earth Observatory at Columbia University. To placate the head of appropriations in the House and Senate, another one would be Iowa's Fish and Wildlife Center, and a fourth, Montana State University. The last project would be at the National Institute of Standards and Technology—NIST, a branch of the U.S. Department of Commerce.

NIST would administer the green building program funds. I later learned that NIST had thousands of employees who did all types of standards and technical development and research; one of their divisions even specialized in construction and the environment. NIST's mission was to reduce the cost of designing and operating buildings and to make the United States more competitive internationally. Unbeknownst to me at the time, NIST would play a big role in my future.

"What's the next step?" I asked Mike. After a short brainstorm on the phone, we agreed that we needed to talk with Terry about our role. We'd help him develop the congressional green building program, but in return, we wanted to be part of it.

After the call, I ripped out and threw away the page with the prospective company names, then read through the notes I'd scribbled while talking with Mike. I made a list of next steps— the first one being formulation of a plan we could pitch to Terry when we called him the following week. Then I went down the hall to tell Jeff the good news. That night, he took me out to cele- brate at Greens, my favorite vegetarian restaurant on the water- front at Fort Mason.

The call with Terry the next week went well—in fact, he seemed very eager to have us work with him. The three of us would form a nonprofit organization to support the congressional demonstration program. Its purpose would be to find green build- ing products for the five buildings. Our goal was to develop a method, based on life cycle assessment (evaluating the environ- mental impact of products over their full life, from materials extraction to reuse or disposition), for selecting green products. I would also provide consulting services to the projects, helping them to define and implement "green."

We hoped manufacturers of green products would join the non- profit as members. To fund the new entity, we'd charge them an initiation fee and annual dues. That part of the plan had particular appeal for me. It had been two months since I'd received a pay- check. I'd also had to make the first payment—of $50,000—to my Arlington partners. My rapidly diminishing resources made me feel both eager and desperate to earn money. I still equated income with success, and it was hard to shake that concept.

We agreed that since I was the only one who was unemployed, I'd become president of the new organization, working full time in Jeff's Battery Street office.

A nonprofit made sense, given the premature business poten- tial of the nascent green building field. And as I pulled away from my past, I liked the idealism of being part of a nonprofit, and of somehow leading the way for others. I could also finally devote myself to projects that adopted a fully integrated design approach.

I couldn't believe my eyes when a fax came from Terry's office a month later. It was a copy of the *Congressional Record* reporting the appropriation of $1 million for the green building demonstration program. Terry had pulled it off! Amazed, I sat in my office with a big smile plastered on my face, feeling like a kid after his first ride without training wheels.

During the next month I rose at 6 A.M. and hit the phone at the office by 7. I was calling building product manufacturers, asking them to become part of our nonprofit and to include their products in the congressional demonstration program projects. The five projects and federal government linkage served as our bait to get them interested. Without this link, we'd never have tried to create the nonprofit. To get their attention, I'd fax the firms a copy of the *Congressional Record*. A few of the people I'd contacted pointed out that the congressional program did not mention our nonprofit and asked if we had an agreement with the program and any of the five projects. I could honestly say yes. Terry was the key to it all—his clients' buildings, the $200,000 planning grants that each would receive, and his influence in Congress. He was already working on getting more funding, with the goal of $10 million in the next round.

I'd printed temporary letterhead on 100 percent postconsumer brownish paper. We named the start-up the U.S. Green Manufacturers Council: The qualifier *U.S.* linked it to the congressional program; our target members were product manufacturers; and the word *council* seemed fitting. I listed Mike, Terry, and myself on the left margin as the company officers. My title was President; Mike's was General Counsel, and Terry's, Vice President. We'd agreed that any start-up expenses would be paid out of future member dues. In my eagerness, I'd ignored my basic business judgment by failing to stipulate that the three of us would pony up equally for the expenses until we collected the money. Instead, I was the only one reaching into my pocket. As my monthly outlay increased, I became anxious. Mike and Terry never offered to help, and I didn't push it. My future depended on this working out. All my chips were on the table.

I looked for major manufacturing firms that had demonstrated environmental leadership. When I found a candidate, I'd mail, fax, call, and FedEx them until they agreed to meet with us or told me to bug off. I considered both responses a success. At least I was casting my fly to a fish.

In December 1992 I flew out to visit Terry's clients, Columbia University's Lamont Doherty Earth Observatory and the New England Aquarium. Terry had asked me to help them write their $200,000 planning grant applications, which had to be sent to NIST for approval. I came up with a green program for each of them. Columbia was planning a new laboratory building, and the aquarium wanted to expand and upgrade its outdated existing facility in Boston, at Central Wharf. These projects included setting performance guidelines in various areas of green building: energy, water, materials, waste, and indoor environmental quality. Since there were no national green building standards, I used our ASTM Green Building Subcommittee draft standard. I also incorporated the idea of a "green team" of outside experts—architects, planners, energy engineers, materials scientists, and air quality experts—who would guide the projects and, we hoped, would join the nonprofit as another membership category.

On my visit to the Lamont Doherty Earth Observatory campus, each morning I woke up early, feeling invigorated. Their mission appealed to me: "To understand how planet Earth works, in all of its physical manifestations . . . Providing a scientific basis for the difficult choices faced by humankind in its stewardship of our planet." The 125-acre wooded campus, located along the Hudson in Palisades, New York, employed over two hundred scientists and graduate students from all over the world. I sat with them in the mess hall and played ping-pong with them at night. I'd never met people who cared so passionately about our Earth's future. At night I'd lie awake in my dorm room staring at the ceiling. Was it possible that I'd been able to change my life so much in just a few months? The nausea and discontent I'd felt on arriving in San Francisco waned as I soaked up the pure air all around me.

As I moved along the windy paths connecting the various academic buildings on campus, I thought back to conversations some of my collegues and I had in the office in D.C. during my development days. "How much do you think we'll clear on this building sale after expenses and payoff of the loan?" "What do you think about the new BMW 7 series versus the Mercedes 500 SEL? I'm having a hard time choosing." At that time, of course, in the back of my mind I was calculating everything in terms of monetary and status value. Yet here, I'd overheard—and sympathized with—two scientists muttering in disbelief over rampant clear-cutting of trees in the Amazon rainforest and the increase in global warming.

Both clients ended up getting a $200,000 planning grant from NIST. I told myself that my turn would come soon. After all, I'd written those two NIST applications; it was only a matter of time before I would be introduced to the other three demonstration projects. With only a few green buildings in the country, these five constituted a quantum leap. I'd gain valuable experience by the end of the demonstration program. My future in the new field of green building would be secure.

CHAPTER 7

Starting the Council

FOR THE NEXT THIRTEEN WEEKS, I hit my desk by seven, with two cups of strong coffee already jangling through my arteries. Coffee was an awful substitute for sleep. My eyes were swollen, with large bags under them. I even skipped exercise during that time. The jeans I'd bought at Gap a month ago were getting tighter and tighter. My hair was long and bushy, on its way to becoming an afro. Piles of papers and packages to be mailed to prospective members covered every surface of my office.

One morning, as I was sifting through my calling list for new members, the phone rang. "Hello," I mumbled. My lips felt frozen.

"It's Joe Smecker from Milliken. I'm returning your call." My pulse quickened. I'd called Joe three times, trying to get him to fly to D.C. to meet with Mike and me in mid-January 1993.

"Jooooe, tanks for caalllling," I managed to get out. What was happening to me? Was I having a heart attack? I thought my chest or arm was supposed to hurt, but other than my mouth freezing up and being unable to speak, I felt fine—well, except for a racing pulse, as if my heart was in overdrive. And a twitching hand. After trying for a few more minutes to speak, without success, I finally managed to convey to Joe that I'd call him back.

Without another thought, I packed up my things, drove home, climbed into bed, and slept for the entire afternoon.

The next day I was back at my desk at seven. My only concession was to lay off the coffee for a while. I never did learn what happened to me. If I'd been less driven, I might have gone to see a doctor, but I didn't have the time. Getting sick or slowing down was not part of my game plan. I had a mountain to climb, and nothing was going to get in my way.

At the end of that period, I took the red-eye to Washington. I'd lined up meetings over the next two days with five global manufacturing firms. Mike and Terry would join me.

The plane's wheels touching down at Dulles International Airport jolted me awake. I rubbed the sleep from my eyes and put on my jacket and dark-green full-length wool Hugo Boss overcoat from my developer days. On the Dulles Access Road, my taxi passed one of the projects I'd managed for Z Development. I noticed that they had new signs posted, listing a new development company. No doubt they'd fired the last one. I'd heard Karen had made millions when they successfully sued their lawyers for negligence. By the time the taxi pulled up in front of Terry's downtown building on Eye Street, we'd passed several of Jim's construction signs. His business was surviving the down economy, but he'd had to go through several rounds of layoffs. As for me, I still wasn't rich, but I was working at doing good.

Terry's firm, the Wexler Group, occupied the entire sixth floor at the modern office building. The elevator was crowded, yet all the passengers, men and women, looked as if they'd shopped at the same clothiers: They wore dark-blue or charcoal-gray suits with starched white shirts, even the women, the more daring of whom had a two-tone scarf draped around their shoulders. I thought about what they would wear back home in California:

shorter skirts without panty hose, and lots of color and skin showing. Most would have tans and look fitter. When I lived in D.C.
people thought cool was pulling an all-nighter at work or working
at the White House; in the Bay Area it meant doing something
like the Escape from Alcatraz triathlon: a one-and-a-half-mile
swim through the bay's frigid waters, eighteen-mile bike ride
through the hills, and an eight-mile run through the Presidio.

Terry's firm had its own lobby—marble floors with oriental
rugs, original art, an enormous floral arrangement, and deep
leather chairs. I took a seat. I was early and Mike wasn't there yet.
I looked at the wall of photos. There was Anne Wexler with
Jimmy Carter; underneath was a handwritten note from the president. The main phone was ringing off the hook while the recep-
tionist struggled to keep up. The pace was definitely faster than on
the West Coast.

Just as Terry came out to greet me, Mike walked into the lobby.
We all shook hands. Terry was about my height, five foot ten, with
thinning black hair. His body was wiry, showing his runner's
physique, and he moved with the lightness of an athlete. He wore
a D.C. power suit: dark-gray wool with a thin pinstripe. His shirt
was the latest two-tone—blue with a white collar, his tie was yellow with dark circles, his cuff links large and gold with the
American eagle on each—the ones you get only from someone
high up at the White House.

We settled into three black leather sofa chairs circling a coffee
table in Terry's office. The walls held photos of Terry with various
presidents, congressmen, and other top public officials. On his
desk were pictures of his wife and two small children. Out the
window I saw the White House a few blocks away. I smiled. It felt
good to be affiliated with Terry's world. I sat up straighter, feeling
a sense of purpose course through me. Terry fidgeted in his seat.

His phone rang and he got up to take the call. Mike and I chitchatted while Terry advised a client on the status of a funding request via the latest House appropriations bill. It was as if he was speaking a different language. I was still amazed that Terry could get the government to fund his clients' buildings. That was quite a skill to have on our team.

Terry sat back down, landing heavily in his chair, and took a deep breath. He seemed to be under great stress. He'd told us he had about thirty clients, which seemed like a full load to me. He had rings around his eyes and kept looking around his office, as if he was having trouble concentrating. "I've got some bad news," he said finally. Mike and I sat forward in our chairs.

"What's up?" Mike asked. I held my breath.

"I'm out." He slapped his knee

"What do you mean, you're *out?*" I asked. My pulse was racing and my body temperature felt as if it had risen twenty degrees in the past few seconds.

"I've got a conflict. I can't represent Columbia University and the New England Aquarium and also be an officer of an organization whose purpose is to sell its members' products to my clients' buildings." Terry's shoulder was toward us, his legs pointed away. I clasped both hands into fists.

"That's it?" Mike asked. "Just like that?" He spoke slowly, trying to make sense of what he'd just heard. Sweat pricked the back of my neck. My adrenal glands were pumping as if I were marching into battle under mortar attack.

"I'm sorry," Terry said. "I have no choice." He walked over to his desk, indicating that the meeting was over. I stood up; Mike had already begun walking to the door. There was so much I wanted to say to Terry. Instead, I followed Mike out of Terry's office.

How could I have been so dumb? My father had urged me to get a written agreement from Terry and Mike, but I'd decided to trust that it would all work out. Had Terry masterminded all of this from the start? I felt betrayed, especially since he had recognized his conflict only after I'd spent several weeks and two trips helping his clients get the $200,000 grants, making him look good. Columbia hadn't even reimbursed my travel expenses, and neither client had paid me for my time. Mike was fine—he was a partner in a law firm. But I was thousands of dollars out of pocket in expenses, not to mention lost salary, for the new organization. If this didn't work, I'd go broke.

We still had five meetings scheduled the next day with product manufacturers at Mike's office. Most of them were flying in to meet with us. What would we tell them, I asked Mike as we left the building.

"Let's just tell them the truth," Mike said. He showed a mouthful of teeth, then laughed. Our plans were in ruins, but he was cheerful. "You've got to love it," Mike said, hitting me on the shoulder. "If you take it too seriously, it'll kill you." I frowned, failing to see his point. "Just remember, we're alive and not in jail," he added.

I only saw the black side of things. Terry was our only connection to the congressional green building program and the five projects that were in the works. That was the main bait for the manufacturers. Why would they join a nonprofit membership organization without that link? They'd be angry that they wasted their time and money coming to meet us. Maybe we could still reach them and cancel, I thought. I could take a late flight home and drown myself in videos on my couch.

The next morning, though, I found myself trudging toward downtown from my friend Reed's house on Ingleside Terrace, where I was staying. We'd worked together during those stressful days at Z Development. It was cold out, with frost on the ground. I pulled my coat collar tight around my face and tugged on my gloves, even as I kept an eye out for strange-looking cars on 16th Street. Reed had told me there was a serial killer running around D.C. shooting people at random with a shotgun. He'd already killed about a dozen. I thought about the relief that might come from becoming his next victim. But then anger surged through me. I wouldn't quit. I was done quitting. I picked up my pace, arriving at Mike's office about twenty-five minutes later.

Soon I was tapping my pen impatiently on the table in Mike's law firm conference room with glass walls, marble rectangular tables, black leather chairs. "It feels as if we're waiting for our own funeral," I said.

His busy eyebrows arched. "It's not so bad. What else would you be doing on such a beautiful morning? Think of it as a great opportunity to learn about human nature." I shook my head. Where'd this guy come from? He looked at me the way my brother Glenn did when I was taking myself too seriously. I cracked a small, painful smile.

Mike's secretary escorted in Joe Smecker, our first meeting. He was the environmental scientist from Milliken, a multibillion-dollar private carpet manufacturing firm, one of the largest and most respected in the world. We stood to shake hands and then all sat around the table. Joe, balding with stringy dark hair, was chubby and a bit bent over. He wore thick glasses that needed a good cleaning, and his dark-blue suit looked as if he'd slept in it. Yet despite his appearance, his eyes radiated intelligence. I'd heard high praise of his leadership as chair of the Carpet and Rug Institute's environmental carpet standard. It had taken me a few months to track him down and develop enough of a rapport to get him to meet with us.

Mike said, "We have some good news and some bad news. Which do you want first?" I bit my lower lip and looked down at my notes, which now seemed like a waste of time.

"Let's start with the good news," Joe said. He had taken out his notepad, but now put his pen down and took off his glasses and began cleaning them.

"Well, the good news is that David and I are here to meet with you."

He shook his head up and down and looked at us like we were a little crazy. "And the bad news?" What on earth was Mike going to say?—we're wasting your time, have a good trip home?

"Our third partner, Terry Bevels with the Wexler Group, resigned last night. He was the link to the congressional projects," Mike said.

"I see." Joe flattened his palm on the table. "What are you guys going to do?"

"We thought we'd get your take on that," Mike said. Joe leaned forward in his chair.

"Tell me what you're thinking."

I blinked in surprise. He was still here.

Mike nodded at me to take over. "Without the projects," I said, "we can broaden our base of members." Inventing my arguments as I went, I explained that when the focus was the five demonstration projects, we thought the council would be composed mostly of manufacturers and a few architects and engineers. Without a tie to the projects, however, we were free to build a more vibrant and integrated membership, one that represented the entire building industry. From my experience as chair of ASTM's Green Building Subcommittee, I'd learned the importance of having all parties at the table. Joe and Mike were nodding.

"The traditional adversarial position of environmentalists and manufacturers is changing," Mike said. "We've found at ASTM that a lot more can be accomplished by working together rather than suing each other."

"The nonprofit will embrace this concept," I added.

"That makes sense to me," Joe said. "We've had the same experience at the Carpet and Rug Institute. Legal action should be a last resort, not a first step." I looked at my watch, amazed that we were still meeting. Joe had even taken a few notes. Earlier I would have bet that he'd already be in a cab headed to the airport by now.

"Demonstration projects are important, but it's even more urgent that we define 'sustainable building' and set guidelines," I said. "There is still mass confusion."

"What do you have in mind?" Joe asked.

"We could help accelerate ASTM environmental building standards," Mike said. "A catalyst organization could shave years off the slow ASTM process by developing the standards in a fast, consensus-based manner." Taking turns, Mike and I went on to describe other programs we could create: a green building resource center, an economic benefits study, and even our own green building rating system, like the one recently inaugurated in England. This was something I was particularly keen on. Rating systems, like the Good Housekeeping Seal and EPA's Green Lights voluntary standard, had helped their respective areas develop rapidly.

"What do you need from us?" Joe asked.

"We'll need your support with other firms," Mike said. "A letter would be great."

"We can do that."

"When we officially form, we'll have to charge dues," I said.

"Of course," Joe said.

"What amount would you pay?" Mike asked.

"Somewhere around $10,000," Joe said easily. "We pay even more to the Carpet and Rug Institute, but it's in our field." I grinned inwardly; Joe had thrown us a life preserver.

Mike and I were smiling as we walked Joe into the lobby and greeted our next appointment, a representative from Herman Miller furniture company, a multibillion-dollar global manufacturer. I had tracked him down at the AIA convention in Boston, where he gave a talk about the firm's progressive environmental wood purchasing guidelines. When we sat down and he asked us how the meeting with Milliken had gone, I felt relieved that Mike could honestly say, "Great." Mike then explained that we saw the exit of Terry and the projects as an opportunity to expand our membership and activities base. When the man nodded, I was elated. We brainstormed the new nonprofit industry council with him, coming up with even more good ideas. At the end of the meeting he, too, agreed to write a letter of support and told us he had no problem paying $10,000 annual dues, plus an initiation fee of $15,000.

By day's end, Mike and I had conducted three more meetings. One firm, Carrier Corporation, not only pledged its support but also said that the company's new head of environmental marketing, Rick Fedrizzi, would make a good founding chairman of our nonprofit. They invited me to meet him a few weeks later at a media event Carrier was hosting in Squaw Valley.

At the end of the day Mike and I retreated to his office, which was cluttered with law books and client papers. A time sheet sat on his desk, and I saw that he hadn't billed a single hour over the past two days. I wondered how his firm felt about the new nonprofit. We later agreed that Mike would earn a monthly fee as general counsel.

I took off my tie and rolled up my shirtsleeves. "We need to get a beer to celebrate," I said. I was all smiles. "And a new name."

"Something tells me you already have an idea." Mike took out his legal pad and picked up a pen.

"I still like the name we came up with when Terry was involved. Let's just make one adjustment, and call it the U.S. Green *Building* Council." We'd drop the word *manufacturers* now that we planned to represent the full array of sectors across the diverse industry.

"And I suppose," Mike said with a chuckle, "you also know where to get the founding members and good office space." My eyes lit up and I smiled.

As I walked back to Reed's for dinner, it was difficult not to run. Despite the winter chill, I felt warmth pulsating through my body. I passed a big construction hole for a new project at McPherson Square. It took up the entire block. Why hadn't I noticed it this morning? I couldn't wait to share my good news with Reed, who just last night had patiently listened to my abject complaining. Then I'd phone home to tell my parents the good news. Now that we had a plan and supporters, I could hold off asking my dad for money. The world was sure looking up.

CHAPTER 8
Phone Calls, Faxes, and Frappuccinos

I FLEW BACK TO SAN FRANCISCO filled with jubilation—and with a new feeling of purpose. Our goal was to formally launch the U.S. Green Building Council four months later, in April 1993. The American Institute of Architects would host the meeting in their D.C. boardroom. Although the AIA hadn't yet agreed to join, having the meeting at the national headquarters implied their support.

Now I had to get us to that goal. Mike and I hoped to have about forty firms in attendance, with at least one firm in each of a dozen categories of our diverse vision of membership for the new coalition. That meant finding leaders from the fields of energy, development, construction, homebuilding, architecture, planning, environmental organizations, government, manufacturing, property management, professional societies, and technical institutes.

I went back to working the phones and the postal meter. To attract new members, I faxed copies of all the letters of support we'd obtained to date. I aimed to create a snowball effect, as Mike had taught me. However, it wasn't always easy to find the right contact at a given firm—in fact, simply identifying which firms to get in touch with could be quite difficult. One of my best methods was to attend the various national conferences and trade expos of the AIA and the Construction Specifications Institute, a membership society of 20,000 technical design professionals involved in the specification of building products and systems. Once I got a person's name, it would go on my hit list. I would then mail an informational package; after that, I would call every other week until they either agreed to write a letter of support and attend the April meeting or told me to leave them alone. I'd used the same method getting firms to meet with Mike and me in January, except now I had turned up the volume.

I met with Kathleen Cruise, a representative of Pacific Gas and Electric, my local utility, who pledged her support. I'd tracked her down because she was the project manager for their Pacific Energy Center on Howard Street. The building showcased energy-efficient lighting and HVAC technologies and hosted industry training programs. She had contacts at Southern California Edison, in Los Angeles, and San Diego Gas and Electric. Soon I was on the phone with them; both representatives were enthusiastic and, after a barrage of my best sales tactics, wrote support letters. Chuck Angyal from SDG&E agreed to join us at the kickoff meeting in D.C. The utilities still had rebate programs to promote energy efficiency, and immediately understood the benefit of supporting our green building agenda.

Another important component of green building was waste minimization. Governmental waste management authorities liked green building because of its emphasis on reducing construction and demolition debris in landfills. Cities couldn't meet their waste reduction goals without using some elements of green building. Construction and demolition debris accounts for over 20 percent of landfill capacity, as I'd learned.

Getting building owners to support us was a greater challenge. They were, understandably, more immediately interested in the bottom line than in saving the planet. In my early public lectures to real estate groups I made the mistake of focusing on the environmental degradation caused by buildings. The feeling in the room was dead. Later I learned to talk only about economic benefits, using the traditional financial analysis I'd relied on as a developer. I realized that for the business sector, what we needed to do was green their greed.

The underlying ethic of all business is profit. This is the entity's responsibility to partners and shareholders. Another given is growth—growth in sales, market extent, number of products, workforce, resource consumption, and profit and net worth. That's America. Trying to fight this is impossible, like trying to move a mountain with a shovel. Building owners will only embrace green building when it is tied directly to their bottom line: rental rates, tenant leasing, lower expenses, higher occupancy rates, greater loan amounts at lower interest rates, higher building sales prices, and improved returns on investment. These parameters are the pulse of the business of real estate and dearest to the owner's heart.

Many environmentalists refused to comprehend this given. Greenpeace may have shifted big corporations a few degrees in their normal course of business by staging dramatic strikes, blocking ships from delivering their goods, and other such efforts, but a more pragmatic approach would be to change how we make money and define financial value.

As we set out to build the council in 1993, we could supply solid information on the financial costs and benefits of energy, water, and waste efficiency. It would take more than a decade to slowly solicit and gather information in other areas of green building, such as occupant health and productivity, and impact on rents, building value, and overall financial return.

It's not easy to affect the momentum of the world's largest industry, which accounts for around $3 trillion globally and some $700 billion in the United States. Such a process of transformation must have many stages and steps, and that takes time and patience—a virtue that I was slowly learning to embrace. My nature was to sprint up the mountain. If someone tried to slow me down or, even worse, stop my rapid ascent, I became frustrated and furious. This personality trait emerged repeatedly as we set out on our dream of creating the council and changing the U.S. building industry. I was, often enough, my own worst enemy as I drove to flatten the hill and defy gravity.

The leading design professionals in architecture, planning, and engineering understood the aims of the council at once. It was fairly common for designers to use natural elements. They understood the wisdom of maximizing day lighting and using solar shading to minimize heat gain during the summer months, and of natural ventilation through operable windows and other measures. And of course, they were adept at adaptive reuse of older structures. Historic preservation is green at its core. Enormous materials and fabrication energy savings can be achieved simply by starting with an existing building. The key, and sometimes a conflicting challenge with the principles of preservation (for example, replacing old inefficient windows with new double-paned ones), is to then retrofit for ongoing resource efficiency and occupant health.

Engineers who were already trying to maximize energy efficiency and enhance air quality and thermal comfort also thought the council was a great idea. The first to jump on board was Alan Traugott with Flack & Kurtz Engineers of New York. His firm had worked on both the NRDC and Audubon projects in Manhattan. Alan had helped me attract more firms to our April launch.

Finding kindred spirits like him made all the difference. To achieve our dream we had to spread our vision. It was like throwing seeds into the wind so they germinate in far-flung fertile fields.

The first environmental organization to sign up was the renowned Rocky Mountain Institute. Bill Browning, head of green development services, had served as my vice chair at ASTM and watched as our plan took shape. "The council is exactly what the country needs," he said when I first explained the idea to him at the end of 1992. "What do you need us to do?"

NRDC was next. I had been referred to one of their lead international energy experts, Rob Watson, by the staff scientist who toured me through their New York building the year before. "This is exactly the type of group we've been looking to join forces with," Rob said during our first conversation. "We have to begin to work closely with industry if we're going to change this world before it's too late."

Having RMI and NRDC, two powerful environmental organizations, on board made an enormous difference. Their names had clout and credibility with the government, manufacturers, and many of our other targeted industry sectors. Politically, they fell in the middle of the environmental movement. Unlike those to the far left, these organizations understood the value of working with manufacturers, even firms that produced toxic products or were on the EPA's Superfund cleanup list. As Bill put it, "If we are going to green the world, we need to show business that green is profitable"—and you couldn't do that by adversarial means.

After Jim's construction company built out the tenant improvements for the Environmental Defense Fund in Washington in 1991, I'd met with one of their senior scientists, Richard Denison. He told me that the year before they had established an environmental partnership with McDonald's Corporation (after having sued them). That collaboration led to a pervasive recycling program, in which McDonald's purchased hundreds of millions of dollars' worth of recycled-content materials for their stores and packaging and diverted thousands of tons of waste from the landfill. The recycling effort not only helped environmentally, but it also saved McDonald's considerable amounts of money. By working with an enlightened industry leader, EDF was able to create a new market overnight. I never forgot this important lesson, and tried to use it in our formation of the USGBC.

In essence, Mike and I had invented a new way of doing business as an industry. There was no precedent for such a coalition and its integration across traditional boundaries. Generally, membership within a specific sector was highly restricted. Environmental organizations were never invited to join manufacturer trade associations, for example—and vice versa. What a particular sector did was not open or answerable to broad-based comments or negative votes, such as the consensus voting procedures that we'd followed at ASTM, and that we intended to bring to the council.

All told, most industry trade organizations were essentially lobbyists. I had a visceral reaction to many of them. The mere definition of lobbying meant trying to influence legislators in favor of special interests, whether or not they were good for the environment. Our vision, in contrast, was to build an organization of leaders who demonstrate constructive action through bricks-and-mortar methods: by constructing buildings that optimize environmental performance and are healthy for occupants and the planet.

As firm after firm signed up to attend the kickoff meeting, I felt invigorated. I carried their support letters around in my briefcase as if they were priceless heirloom jewelry passed down by my grandmother. Each letter that came in renewed my sense of commitment.

Money continued to be a problem, though. I was still working without pay and writing checks to cover the council's bills. I felt more desperate as my bank account continued its steady slide. For the first time in my life, I stopped eating out, opting to fix meals at home. Buying new clothes was out of the question. I'd even driven to L.A. to visit my folks instead of flying.

"You'll starve." The words of my father when I'd set out on this journey reverberated late at night in my head. Whenever I heard it, I'd get out of bed, get dressed, and head to the office to send out more faxes and prepare more mailings. At 5 A.M. I'd be on the phone, calling people as they arrived at their East Coast offices. "What are you doing up at this hour?" one man asked me. "Are you crazy?"

Mike continued working full time at his law firm. "You're doing a great job, David. I don't know how you do it," he'd say before giving me a list of a few more people to contact. His support and creative enthusiasm were important, but I still felt isolated and somewhat insecure without proper funding, staff, and a committed board and membership.

I knew I'd feel a lot better when we had a chairman to legitimize our nascent organization. Mike and I wanted to recruit a progressive leader from a global manufacturing firm. In late January 1993, after our encouraging round of meetings in D.C., I trekked out to Squaw Valley to meet Rick Fedrizzi, director of environmental marketing at Carrier Corporation. I knew the hundred-year-old firm from my construction and development days; it was the world's largest manufacturer of heating, ventilating, and air conditioning products, with forty thousand employees in 170 countries. Its parent company was United Technologies Corporation, a top-fifty U.S. corporation with annual revenues of

$25 billion. UTC also owns Otis Elevator, Pratt & Whitney, Hamilton Sundstrand, and Sikorsky.

Rick had helped his company adapt their products to reduce ozone depletion, boost energy efficiency, improve indoor air quality, and reduce packaging. The Squaw Valley meeting was an environmental press briefing on their products for about forty trade publications.

When I finally tracked Rick down, he was decked out in ski clothing: dark-blue overalls, black after-ski boots, a multicolored sweater. About forty years old, six foot four, with sparkling deep-green eyes, he looked like an oversized teddy bear. His warmth and approachability reminded me my two brothers. Over a beer at the lodge, he told me that as the father of two young children, he was starting to look more broadly at his life purpose. "My kids love this stuff," he remarked with regard to his environmental role at Carrier. "It's the first time they've ever taken an interest in my work." When I told Rick why I was there, his response was enthusiastic but tentative: "I don't know what it means to be chairman of a nonprofit. But I'd like to learn more." Clearly, I would need to do further explaining. And what better place than on the slopes at Squaw?

"I've only skied at Syracuse with my kids," Rick said the next day as we rode the chairlift to the top of the mountain. We'd been warming up on blue runs, chatting on the lift rides up about the USGBC and his potential role as our first chairman. Now, though, it was time for a more serious workout. "I do the black diamonds in Syracuse, but they're not nearly this steep," he said, as he eyed the steep mogul run beneath us. It looked fun to me. I was eager to test the soft demo skis I'd just rented at the hotel's posh shop.

"I'm sure it'll be no problem," I said with a grin. Rick tightened his grip on the safety bar.

We got off the lift and I egged him on toward the easiest black diamond slope. I'd grown up skiing at Mammoth Mountain with my brothers. We'd been to Squaw Valley several times as a family—flying there in my father's plane. Mom and Dad also liked to ski. Once I had to ski down KT22, one of the steepest and iciest runs at the resort, carrying Glenn's skis. He'd fallen at the top and slid halfway down before coming to an abrupt halt—at the expense of a dislocated shoulder.

"You can do it," I urged Rick, who stood staring down the vertical face, the tips of his skis barely protruding over the edge of the run. "It gets easier as you gain momentum," I shouted as I jumped off and made a turn into the soft powder. This was my first run of the year, and it felt great to be skiing again. Rick ultimately overcame his fears and proceeded slowly but steadily to make his way down the mountain. His form was good and his legs strong. I made a few more turns, then waited for him at the bottom.

"That was fantastic," he said with a smile as big as the mountain. "I was thinking about the council on my way down. I'd like to be the founding chairman."

"Fantastic." I sidestepped a few paces up the mountain to shake his hand and pat him on his big, parka-encased shoulder.

The truth is that none of us had the experience to design and construct what we dreamed of building. As in a steep mountain climb, our strategy was to gather a balanced and inspired team and the necessary gear, and simply set out on the journey. We tried not to focus on the height of the mountain or the ruggedness of the terrain, but just to progress, one step at a time. Of course, we were doing it where there were no trails, because nobody had been up this particular mountain before. We were building the first industry coalition of its type in the world. The key was to keep our sights on the top and never stop climbing or look down—which in practical terms meant working to change the way we designed, financed, constructed, and operated our buildings in order to minimize their ecological footprint on the planet. What we didn't understand was that in changing our relationship to the world, we would also change ourselves.

Even though Mike's and my decision to appoint Rick as chairman was quick, almost intuitive, over the next decade, our faith in him was validated many times over. Rick provided exactly the leadership and strength of character and vision that we needed. He was also the perfect foil to Mike and me, with our hot tempers and brash manner. In those days, if we didn't like someone, we labeled them "darksider" and plotted over drinks how to "take them out." If Rick was present, he'd calm us down and get us to agree to release our aggression by laughing more over drinks or going out for a run with him. Through his solidity and evenness, mixed with vision and insight, he got the best out of us, stabilizing us and goading us onward. He went on to become the peacemaker for the council as our momentum increased and we began to encroach on sacred turfs on all sides. We couldn't have found a better leader than Rick.

Finally, April 1993 rolled around. We had sixty firms confirmed for the kickoff meeting of the council and a stack of support letters from leaders in a dozen sectors of the building industry.

Once the taxi had dropped me at AIA's headquarters on New York Avenue, I straightened my green-patterned tie and tried to smooth the airplane wrinkles from my trusty green suit. I ran my fingers through my hair. It was longer than when I lived in D.C. My hairline had begun to recede, but no gray yet. Glasses wouldn't come until later. I was thirty-two.

I hurried into the building and headed upstairs to the boardroom. Caterers were setting up a continental breakfast in the reception area outside. Should I eat something? No. My stomach was unsettled. Although it was a decade since my first negotiation in a very different boardroom, I had the same fears. Would they take me seriously? Would I be able to find my voice at the podium and convey the leadership strength of a president? My notes, with three-colored highlighting, burned a hole in my pocket. I'd reviewed them so thoroughly on the plane that the paper was worn at the edges. Would I return home as president of a new nonprofit organization? Would the attendees agree to become members and fund us?

It seemed of utmost importance. If we could change the thinking of the world's largest industry in the most consumption-oriented country, we might be able to ensure a more sustainable life for future generations. At the end of my Washington days, Jim's firm had been involved in the building of the U.S. Holocaust Memorial Museum. On the front of the building are inscribed these words: *"First they came for the Socialists, and I did not speak out—because I was not a Socialist. Then they came for the trade unionists, and I did not speak out—because I was not a trade unionist. Then they came for the Jews, and I did not speak out—because I was not a Jew. Then they came for me—and there was no one left to speak out for me."* It was our generation's time to speak out against the destruction of the planet, and I hoped I'd be heard loud and clear.

The stakes were high for me personally, too. I'd put everything I had into the council. It was my best creation, with the greatest potential of anything I'd ever done. What if they didn't want it?

I entered the boardroom, and something in me relaxed when I saw Mike already there, setting up the overhead projector. He looked up and saw me. "Hey, David. Ready for the show?" His broad smile flashed white teeth. His black hair—less of it every time I saw him—was parted and slicked back. He was about forty-five but moved around the front of the room with the vitality of someone a dozen years younger. I cracked a wan smile and tried to say yes, but the word caught in my throat. My legs felt heavy.

Soon people began to arrive, and after helping themselves to breakfast and socializing some, everyone poured into the board-room. Mike and I stood together up front as Carl Costello, the director of AIA's Committee on the Environment offered words of welcome. Then we were on.

"Welcome to the founding organizational meeting of the U.S. Green Building Council," Mike began. "Today is the start of a revolution in how we make buildings." As he spoke, I looked out at the attendees, recognizing about half of them. The others I knew only by the sound of their voice. It was a professional group, the men dressed in suits and ties and the women in skirts with scarves and dark blazers. A couple of guys were wearing jeans. I guessed they were from the Environmental Defense Fund and Audubon; they'd agreed to come only last week when I told them that Rocky Mountain Institute and NRDC were already on board. Rick, sitting up front, winked at me. My buddy Reed, a real estate developer, was off to the left; I lifted my chin at him gratefully. I saw Chuck Angyal from San Diego Gas & Electric sitting in the back; he'd already loosened his tie and rolled up his sleeves. He and the guy next to him, Alan Traugott from Flack & Kurtz Engineers, were laughing, probably at one of Chuck's jokes. A chill of excitement shot up my spine. I'd gotten them here! They had come because they believed in our vision, and in me. I could feel the collective electricity of the participants, like the beginning of a thunderstorm just before bolts of lighting flash through the sky.

Then it was my turn. I took a deep breath and began. "Your presence here," I said, "makes you visionaries of a new move-ment—Green Building. We are honored to welcome all of you, representing about a dozen sectors of the industry. Although our council will comprise individual voices that function indepen-dently, together we'll be an orchestra, speaking with one inte-grated and holistic voice for the industry. Our mission will be to transform building design, construction, and operation from con-ventional practices to sustainable ones that optimize profit for both business and the environment." I paused to catch my breath and take the pulse of the room. Several people nodded. Everyone was paying attention.

When I'd finished, Mike returned to the podium. "This is going great," he whispered as we exchanged places. He then launched into the first of his two white papers on recommended council activities. Calm and poised, he walked the group through several overhead slides. The first paper had to do with accelerating ASTM green building standards. We believed the council could inde-pendently develop critical standards at a fast pace, and then intro-duce them into ASTM as appropriate. Mike's second paper was on the concept of developing green product standards for the build-ing industry. It was difficult for product specifiers to determine the pertinent green product attributes and then obtain comparative information from manufacturers, and our thought was that the council could take a leadership role in this area.

I then presented two papers I'd written. One was on the need for us to develop a building rating system—like England's BRE (Building Research Establishment) Environmental Assessment Method, or BREEAM, which had been introduced in 1990 and was now beginning to make a market impact, having been used to certify about 5 percent of new commercial office buildings. (Although Canada was developing a rating system too, it was complicated and unlikely to be accepted by the marketplace.) My second paper was on establishing a green building resource center. As I'd found while working for my cousins, it was a full-time job to track down and assemble information on green building. We could be a one-stop green building informational clearinghouse.

The paper presentations were greeted with warm applause. Mike and I then cleared our throats for the most crucial item on the agenda: organizational formation, including membership and dues. I was determined not to let anyone out of the room until they agreed to join our coalition.

We launched into the topic by introducing the first year's budget, which included staffing—myself as president and Mike as our outside general counsel—and the expense of our headquarters in San Francisco. Next, an overhead slide showed our proposed dues levels. We planned to limit membership to organizations, thus avoiding individual members, who in other organizations paid lower dues, yet required the same level of service in terms of mailing costs, staff time, and meeting costs (including food and room charges). According to our scheme, product manufacturers with revenues of over $1 billion would pay $10,000 annually, plus an initiation fee of $15,000. At the lowest end, but still having the same vote and organizational representation, were environmental nonprofits, with annual dues of $300 and no initiation fee. All other dues fell between $500 and $5,000 depending on a firm's category of membership and organizational size. Payment of all fees up-front would allow us to rapidly capitalize the new group.

Mike stood up. "And now I'd like to take a vote on the formation of the U.S. Green Building Council," he said. "All those in favor, raise your hands."

Standing at the podium alongside Mike, I felt as if my heart had stopped. Silence fell over the room. On the far side of the wall a cart creaked and dishes rattled. I looked, and all over the room hands were reaching toward the sky. Joy and relief hit my backbone. I almost staggered. "Yes! Thank God," I whispered to myself. I felt my face break into a smile the size of the Grand Canyon. As for Mike, he was grinning as if he'd just set foot on top of Mount Everest. I knew how he felt, because I felt the same — though I felt more like I was the first one *ever* to reach the top.

CHAPTER 9

Building the Organization

THE GAME WAS ON. "The goal is to collect $100,000 by the end of June," I said to the group at the founding meeting. "If not, we'll return the money." That meant I had sixty days to collect and deposit the pledged dues in the bank—a difficult task even for a skilled fundraiser at an established nonprofit organization.

That first weekend back from D.C., I switched all the inefficient incandescent lightbulbs in my apartment to compact fluorescents and installed water-saving devices in my sinks, shower, and toilets. Recycling I'd done since I moved in.

On Monday morning, I rose with the sun. I bolted down the three flights of stairs from my apartment and opened up my garage door. The morning light glared off the BMW I'd bought during my developer days. I couldn't drive that anymore. I dusted off my bike, pumped up the tires, and pedaled off downtown to work.

As I rode through the Marina Green I reveled in the fresh morning air. Beyond the furled masts of the boats in the harbor, the water in the bay was calm. Seagulls hovered, occasionally plunging into the water in hopes of catching their morning breakfast. Could I do it? Could I climb the mountain in sixty days? Would the attendees at our kickoff meeting really cut a check and join an organization with no programs, no track record, no official office, no money—just me as the staff, a man with no nonprofit experience whatsoever?

Hitting the grassy hill leading up to Fort Mason, I shifted into my lowest gear, popped out of the seat, and stood on the pedals to pump my way up the incline. I'd do it just like this, pedal stroke by pedal stroke. Soon I'd crested and was zooming down the hill toward Aquatic Park. Fishermen were already out on the long pier, and dedicated cold-water swimmers with little red caps were doing their laps. I felt the exhilaration of speed and wind on my face.

Over the next weeks, I expanded the target list to include firms that had previously expressed interest but were unable to attend the founding meeting. I brought in a temp to help with the mailings. Stacks of packages ready to mail teetered on every surface. Slowly, the list of those who said they would sign up grew.

I flew to Chicago for AIA's national convention: two days to hit three hundred booths in a room the size of several football fields. First I sat down and highlighted the names of large product manufacturers that I knew could contribute to green building—makers of energy systems and of products that could contain recycled content, such as drywall and carpeting, or those that impacted air quality (paint, glues, laminates)—*and* that could pay our $10,000 dues and $15,000 up-front fee.

"Is your product environmental?" I asked the sales representative for Southwall Technologies. I knew that they made an energy-efficient coated film.

"Of course," he said. "We have a new product: Heat Mirror. Have you heard of it?"

I pulled out a small pocket notebook and wrote down the company and product name. The salesman described its energy efficiency properties, giving me a lecture on windows as well.

Apparently, Heat Mirror was developed by NASA to protect astronauts from the sun's radiation. The thin film is placed in the center of two panes of glass and enclosed with krypton gas. It minimizes heat gain and loss while maximizing insulation. He showed me the National Fenestration Rating Council seal for a window with Heat Mirror encased in the middle, certifying its properties. The NRFC had done for windows what we wanted to do for entire buildings: created an accepted national certification system. I launched into my spiel, linking my sales pitch to his product, then handed him a newly printed council brochure and my card. It listed my new title: president. The address was still 901 Battery Street, San Francisco—Jeff's space. I was hoping we could move into our own green space once I collected more than $100,000. I had started compiling a list of manufacturers I wanted to hit up for product donations. I made a note to add Southwall Technologies to the list.

When I got back home, footsore, having given my sales pitch hundreds of times, I sent out a mailer to the new list of targets. Then, as usual, I followed up with phone calls, faxes, and a second round of mailings. I did use a lot of paper, but at least it was environmentally friendly paper, and our brochures used nothing but the finest soy inks.

By the end of June, I had raised $125,000. The council was a reality.

I could now draw a salary and hire staff. The first thing I did was bring on Lynn Simon as a full-time staff member, giving her the role of program manager. Shortly after we'd launched the council, several people encouraged me to track Lynn down. Not only had she been president of the AIA's national student organization under an environmental banner and started the San Francisco

AIA's Committee of the Environment, but she'd also mastered in architecture with a thesis on sustainable design. She was perfect for our first hire, and to this day is still an active board member and officer of the council. We then hired a designer to develop the council logo, hoping that in time it would be considered a brand or seal: two concentric circles with an oak leaf floating in an olive-green background.

Mike and I had handpicked the council's founding board of directors based on the individuals' enthusiasm and the type of organization they represented. We wanted at least one representative from each of our dozen sectors, a goal that took us years to achieve. Our board and about forty organizational members provided testimonials and help with the recruiting process. Our top priority was additional capitalization (through memberships) of our increasing overhead. Rick brought in two large manufacturers, including Johns Manville, the insulation company, which was a supplier to Carrier.

Shortly after our official launch we received checks from two trade organizations, each for $300—the same fee our environmental organizations paid. Although on paper both groups were nonprofits, one represented two thousand firms, and the other about two dozen billion-dollar powerhouse corporations. Mike and I moved quickly to get our board to prohibit trade associations from becoming members, and returned the two checks. If they joined, we feared we'd never recruit any of their members; not only that, but their strategy might snowball to other building product areas, such as carpet, drywall, and wood. If that occurred, USGBC would become a council of trade organizations, killing the pioneering spirit that our visionary and progressive corporate members stood for.

The going was not always easy. "Aren't you primarily an organization of product manufacturers?" Terry McDermott, CEO of the national AIA, asked Mike and me at a meeting in 1994. He'd just been brought in after serving as president of Cahners Publishing to clean house at the AIA, and we'd approached him about partnering in the area of sustainable building. McDermott stiffly extended his hand when we were introduced, smiling in a way that showed his top teeth only. I perched on the edge of my seat, tapping my right foot under the table. "I've heard a lot about your new group. Tell me about your mission," he said as the meeting began. I explained that we were an open and balanced coalition of the entire building industry. "What's your dues structure?" he asked. I told him the amounts were distributed according to the sector's ability to pay, as well as tiered according to an organization's size.

McDermott listened skeptically. "Who pays the most?"

"Large product manufacturers with sales over a billion pay an annual fee of $10,000," I said. "But they only get one vote, same as an environmental organization paying $300. All parties have agreed to this structure, and it's working." I pointed out that we had about eighty firms, only about 20 percent of which were manufacturers. It's true that I'd spent more time recruiting big firms because of the greater financial contribution, but others joined more readily, therefore keeping our membership in balance. (I later heard from several parties that the AIA and some other groups had the perception that we had millions of dollars in our coffers, and were primarily an organization of manufacturers whose goal was to lower the standards for green products—a ploy that we called "green wash.")

McDermott remained unconvinced. I felt my heat rising. "What will be the role of architects in your group? I see that the

AIA San Francisco has joined," he said, the mild form of the question doing little to mask the insinuation it contained. While the national AIA had been deliberating on whether to offer us their support, Lynn Simon had helped me recruit Bob Jacobvitz, the executive director of AIA's San Francisco chapter. He'd even hosted our first San Francisco board meeting in 1993 at his office on Sutter Street.

"We have thirteen sectors of membership. Architects only represent one category," Mike offered. "We also have another category for professional societies. Both ASID [the American Society for Interior Designers] and ASLA [the American Society of Landscape Architects] have joined." He paused. "We'd like the AIA to come on board too. We're open to a reciprocal membership."

McDermott shuffled together the various documents we'd given him. "We'll stay in touch," he said as he rose. It took all my will to extend my hand to shake his on my way out. I couldn't look him in the eye, and instead studied the wood floor.

Meetings like this one, steered by a man of strength and authoritative style, triggered me. At times like these, I immediately felt like the rejected son. It was classic projection. And so, shedding about twenty years' worth of maturity, my only recourse was to stomp out of McDermott's office, hoping he'd notice my anger. I shake my head now to imagine what he must have thought as the head of the USGBC comported himself like an overwrought teenager.

In early 1994 we signed the lease for a new office space, to be built out in a building being renovated on Sansome Street, part of the Transamerica Building complex, overlooking a beautiful little urban park with a waterfall. The landlord agreed to house us temporarily in an adjacent building until the construction was finished.

That gave us time to design our own green space and solicit product donations from our members. I couldn't wait to sit in Herman
Miller's new award-winning, ergonomic Aeron chair and use their
executive stand-up adjustable desk. U.S. Gypsum agreed to give us
the drywall, and Armstrong the ceiling tile we needed (both had
recycled content). We'd have to install three carpets—by Interface,
Milliken, and Collins & Aikman—to showcase our members' latest
environmental carpet tile. Flack & Kurtz Engineers helped design
superefficient lights, and we were talking to Andersen about
installing their latest windows, with the best energy-efficiency values. Meanwhile, we camped out on an enormous vacant floor. Jeff,
whose own lease had been terminated, came along and staked out
a corner in our temporary space. It was comforting to have him
around, and I was glad I could pay back some of his hospitality.

One of the ideas Mike raised during our early formation was a
pollution tax on building products. Products would be taxed
based on their level of pollution, such as the amount of carbon
dioxide produced in the manufacturing process. If two carpet
tiles, for example, were produced by different processes, the
"greener" carpet would get a tax break. Its "green" determination
would come from a more environmentally enhanced process:
use of recycled-content materials, manufacturing plant energy
derived from solar panels or a fuel cell, or using blankets instead
of cardboard and plastic wrapping for shipping. Many environmental groups, such as World Resources Institute and Redefining
Progress, had been studying the potential market impact of such a
tax. Mike was enthralled by the concept and, once the council
was a reality, had put together a group, made up of some architects, our environmental organization members, and a few others, including Herman Miller, to study its applicability to the
building industry. Theoretically, such a tax break could make a

green alternative cheaper, thus encouraging people to buy it. More sales would then mean more manufacturers going green.

Despite such worthy arguments, most of our members were against the initiative. "It's just too early for us to study this," our vice chairman, Bill King from Armstrong World Industries, said to me privately after a board meeting. He was six feet four, with huge hands and a deep voice, and I was a little afraid of him. His firm was the largest ceiling tile manufacturer in the world. "We haven't even defined green building, much less developed policies and procedures," he said. "You've got to get Mike to cool it."

I had been asking Bill, as well as several other board members from big product companies, to help recruit new members, but they'd been stalling. And when I asked for help raising money, again he'd bring up the pollution tax issue, as well as our lack of proper organizational policies and procedures. That was really just another way of saying that if we'd all voted on it, as was proper procedure, Mike wouldn't have been able to proceed with his ad hoc pollution taxes initiative.

In the early days of the council, we weren't formal; our organizational bylaws were skeletal at best. Mike and I freely launched initiatives and even appointed board members as we saw fit, not holding public elections for officers until after our first three years. If we saw someone who was enthusiastic and showed leadership qualities, we got them on board after checking with each other and sometimes with our chairman, Rick Fedrizzi. We ran the council more like a high-tech start-up than an industry nonprofit. "Speed is quality" was Mike's truism we'd been founded on, and stuck to until we got larger. The idea was to create a groundswell of support and momentum, and then work at adding depth to our breadth of initiatives. Lynn Simon helped in that regard by implementing such program initiatives as researching the viability of a resource center at Southen California Edison's Energy Resource Center, and establishing local government and annual conference committees.

As a result of this hang-loose approach and our own philosophical bent, the board ended up being a collection of mavericks, in an industry that was traditionally conservative and slow to change. Building invests less in research and development than almost any other industry—0.5 percent versus 5.0 percent for high tech. We were out to buck that trend.

I was with Mike on pollution taxes. As he put it, if we didn't take on the hard issues, who would? But it was becoming clear that I had to speak to him. If I didn't, we'd lose our manufacturers on the board and they wouldn't help me raise money—and money was crucial. This was the kind of conflict I was most afraid of. The group came from all sides; the only thing we agreed on was the need to boost the environmental performance of our buildings, thereby saving the environment as well as reducing building operating expenses. How could I keep everybody from disagreeing as their natural inclination toward the left or right surfaced on an issue? If we couldn't get along, the council would be split in two like King Arthur's Round Table.

One morning when I was in D.C. for meetings, Mike and I went for a bike ride in Rock Creek Park. He had on cut-off jeans, an old Syracuse University T-shirt, and dirty tennis shoes. I was decked out in black lycra biking shorts, a multicolored Pearl Izumi jersey, Shimano shoes, and yellow mirrored Oakley sunglasses. His bike looked as if it had spent the last thirty years stacked with a lot of other junk in his garage.

I led the way, being more familiar with the trails. Every time I looked back, Mike was right behind me, even though I'd been biking a lot in the steep hills of Marin.

As my tires crunched over twigs and rocks, I vowed that I'd speak to Mike at our next break. At the top of a hill, I pulled off the trail for a drink from my water bottle. Mike caught up to me and dismounted, then took a long gulp from his bottle of Gatorade. It was hot and humid. Under my helmet my hair was dripping with sweat. "Mike," I said.

"What?" Dirt streaked his face.

Another rider swept by, standing on his pedals as he crested the hill, his helmet a shock of blue and yellow against the dark trees. He lifted a hand, and I did the same. Mike was waiting.

"Nothing." I stuck my bottle back in its holder. "Ready?"

Mike was like a brother to me. I didn't want to hurt his feelings. And I hated the idea of giving in to outside pressure.

As was bound to happen, however, the issue boiled over a few months later, at a quarterly board meeting. Jan Beyea, a senior scientist at the National Audubon Society, had just begun his report on a grant application that they'd been working on for the pollution tax committee, when Bill King interrupted. "Why are we taking this on?" he asked. His eyes were steely behind his large-frame glasses. "We have many other more 'apple pie' priorities."

Several others agreed.

"This is chickenshit!" Jan declared. A new board member, he was responsible for Audubon's pioneering green building in Manhattan. He looked like a professor, with tweed coat and thin strands of hair pasted over a high forehead. Now his face and even his balding pate were bright red. He hit the table with his fist, the thump resounding throughout the room. "If we don't have the guts to take on something as important as pollution taxes, then I quit. None of these folks here are environmentalists; they're just a front for the industry." He started stuffing papers into his briefcase and making his way to the door.

I sat there openmouthed. His display reminded me of Khrushchev pounding the table with his shoe. Several people looked at me. I was there to provide leadership, but I had no idea what to say or why Jan was so angry. To date, we'd made it through all controversies by staying at the table until we resolved our differences. Achieving consensus was one of our sacred values. I willed myself to speak, but nothing came out.

Then Bill Browning jumped up so suddenly his chair tipped over. "Fuck you. I can't believe you'd say that," Bill said. Jan wheeled around to face Bill, whose face was contorted and as crimson as his own. All around the table, mouths dropped open with surprise. Bill was the most soft-spoken person on the board.

Jan reached for the door. A rush of voices remonstrated with him. Jan just shook his head and walked out. We never heard from him again.

I was stunned, and later learned that there was much more to the story. I still am not sure of the truth. Like most misunderstandings, it was likely a gray area. Yet curiously, the feeling that flooded me at the time was gratitude. Unfortunately, Jan, a committed board member, had walked away. But if Bill and Rob Watson (representing our other two environmental organizations) had not stayed at the table, our coalition could have have fallen apart then and there. A decade later I still feel overwhelmed at the willingness of our fellow members to embrace, support, and expand on our vision—for similar incidents did occur, many times over the years, and yet we remained together despite our differences and behind-the-scenes feuds. Those early charter members of the council, who joined when it was hardly more than an idea, were change agents and pioneers across all industry sectors, passionate stewards of the planet and its natural resources. They not only had vision, but the tenacity and will to make our

dream a reality. All my life I had felt like an outsider, never comfortable with any club or society. Here, among the other members
of the council, I experienced a deep sense of belonging, such as I
had never known before.

In late 1993 we held our first annual green building conference, in partnership with the National Institute of Standards
and Technology at their Gaithersburg, Maryland, campus. I
walked around mingling (or simply eavesdropping), and most of
the remarks I overheard were animated as the participants
eagerly shared their thoughts on green buildings. "This is
incredible," one man told another. "I'm the only one in my firm
who cares about sustainability. It's amazing to see all these other
enthusiasts. I'm going to go home and tell my boss that this is
going to be big."

The keynote banquet dinner speakers at the conference were
Bill McDonough and Paul Hawken. Bill shared his thoughts on
waste as our feedstock for new products and on the need to make
things that aren't toxic to people and the planet. It was the first
time many had heard him speak. I noticed many heads bobbing
up and down; a few others stared at the ceiling in complete shock,
and a couple of people left.

When Paul's turn came to speak, he said enthusiastically, "I
love the council's coalition model—there's nothing like it in the
world." A few years later he told me that he thought our open and
integrated sector model of membership would work not only in
greening the building industry, but in greening the business world
more generally. Paul was renowned for his provocative bestseller
Ecology of Commerce, advocating the need for business to lead
the sustainable revolution. Paul went on to cowrite (with Amory
and Hunter Lovins) the next important industry bible, *Natural*

Capitalism. It was encouraging to receive this affirmation from such a towering figure in the movement.

In addition to the AIA, I wanted to bring the Construction Specifications Institute in as a professional society member of the council. (The AIA ultimately joined us the next year by creating a reciprocal membership. In time, our relationship turned into a close affiliation.) While attending a CSI conference in Houston to solicit members, I had learned that they wanted to expand their standard manufacturer product information template to incorporate green characteristics. This was a shift with national implications.

The next year, 1994, I was elated to receive an invitation from Ross Spiegel, an officer of CSI, to address its board at its national convention in San Francisco. I planned to talk off the cuff, presenting the history of the council and making a case for CSI's membership. When I walked into the room, I was shocked by the formality of the setting. About a dozen tables were joined together in a circle. In front of each board member was a microphone and nameplate. It looked like the United Nations.

Fortunately, I was not asked to present first, which gave me time to scribble a few notes and learn the protocol. Each party addressing the board had five minutes. I noticed the speakers handed out a copy of their spoken remarks in advance, then presented a formal reading of the text. A queasy feeling in my stomach told me this was a time I should have been more prepared.

Soon my name was called and I took the visiting presenter's hot seat at the roundtable. To my embarrassment, my voice cracked slightly when I introduced myself, as it had at my Bar Mitzvah twenty years before. I caught my breath, then felt my strength of will kick into gear as I told them about the council's programs. "We'd like to work together with CSI to incorporate the principles of sustainable building into its standard specifications," I finished. I returned to my seat exhausted, with no idea what I'd said.

"You did a good job. They were impressed," Ross told me afterward. "Our president wants you to sit with us at our banquet dinner."

That evening, I climbed up onto the stage and joined the head dinner table. I'd dusted off my tuxedo, bought during my D.C. days; it felt tight, but the color was right—nice and black. Seated below us were thousands of CSI members (eight thousand had attended the convention). Would USGBC ever fill such an enormous room?

The president of CSI, William Riesberg, spoke, lauding the work being carried out by Ross and his environmental committee. "And to further our environmental commitment, we will be joining the U.S. Green Building Council as a charter member," he announced before the thousands—to my utter surprise. Ross looked over at me and winked. I simply beamed.

Ross ultimately became a board member of the council, bringing not only his depth of knowledge in the greening of building plans and specifications, but also his decades of organizational experience. He served as our parliamentarian and beacon for organizational professionalism. He would have made Bill King from Armstrong proud, but Bill had retired, having been replaced by Steve Piguet, a baby boomer like me and much easier to work with. The council went on to form a long-term partnership with CSI, cosponsoring several trade expos, which boosted our credibility. Ross further accelerated the environmental platform for both organizations when he became CSI's president in 2001. He also coauthored a book on environmental specifications that further solidified his leadership in the green building movement.

I continued to send out new membership packages and call prospective firms, but after the first rush of charter members, only a fraction of the building industry seemed open to our message. Finding the right contact at the right firm was like panning for gold. The big money lay in bringing in large manufacturers, but the recruiting process for that was difficult and slow. It had taken me a year to enlist several of our latest members. Dozens of others were on the sidelines watching to see if we'd fold or continue to grow.

It was March 1994. I'd increased our overhead significantly since funds started coming in the preceding June. I'd hired Lynn and an assistant, and was trying to pay myself a full salary plus benefits—though that had worked only for the first few months (for the past six I'd been paid nothing). Mike's law firm, billed monthly for his services as general counsel, but we also accrued their payment. The travel budget added up as I flew around the country to attend board meetings, deliver speeches, and continue new member recruiting at big conference trade shows.

At every council board meeting and during officers' conference calls, I brought up our sinking finances. "Let us know who to call and what to say," people would say. But this was not the way to get new recruits. Even the best-intentioned board members were reluctant to make solicitation calls. "David, you're the best at bringing in members," Robert Bell, of U.S. Gypsum, the largest drywall company in the world, said at one board meeting. I would update them on our progress at meetings, and they'd give me a round of applause. I'd smile for a moment and then tense up, thinking of the two-weeks-overdue office rent and our accumulating debts. Every month I paid a fraction on each bill from a long list, trying to remain in good standing. I'd begun to feel a little desperate, especially when I found myself writing a personal check to cover council expenses.

Eventually the council owed me over $70,000 in expenses and unpaid salary, and the bills were still piling up. I decided to take the weekend off, and went up to Mt. Shasta to do some fishing. I pitched my dome tent at the Ah-di-na Campground along the McCloud River, just up from the Nature Conservancy land. I assembled my four-piece Orvis fly rod, put on my waders, dirty boots, and old green vest, and made my way, a wading staff in my other hand, through the trees and into the swiftly flowing river.

I worked my way upstream, casting as I went. The night of mountain air and morning of focused fishing gave me perspective on my situation. By the time I packed up my tent, sleeping bag, and gear and drove home on Sunday, I'd made my decision.

In April I flew to D.C. for a board meeting. This time, as I walked off the plane, my eyes were on the tarmac, not in the clouds. I was no longer wearing "rose-colored glasses."

Once in the boardroom, I passively shook hands with my cohorts. I did not work the room as I had in the past (pumping members with information about our progress and growth). I'm sure everybody there was aware that something had changed in me.

I told them about the dismal state of our finances. "The council can't afford someone at my salary level of $100,000 a year," I said.

"What are you saying?" Bill King asked quietly.

"I have to step down." I took a deep breath and exhaled for several long seconds. Disappointing people who relied on me tore at my insides. "We'll also have to close the San Francisco office and move our operations to D.C."

The board members exchanged glances. The silence felt like the aftermath of a bomb. I stared at a painting on the wall. It depicted a small whaling ship heading into an enormous wave;

the seamen were being thrown all over the boat, but kept hold of a large whale they'd harpooned.

"How will we manage the council's operations?" asked Nevel DeHart, our treasurer. He was president of American Formulating and Manufacturing, a San Diego company that provided a complete range of chemically responsible building and maintenance products.

"Mike has spoken with Tom Cohn. He ran a small management company that could take over under his supervision, for a quarter of our monthly expense." I feared that Tom wouldn't be able to keep up the level of board and member handholding that we'd provided, but I said nothing.

At Rick's suggestion, the board voted me a vice chairman (instead of president) and lifetime board member. They gave me a round of applause for the work I'd done on the council's behalf, and pleaded with me not to abandon my commitment now that I was a dues-paying volunteer. I nodded, but inside I felt deflated.

Immediately after this meeting, I flew to Los Angeles, where my dad was in the hospital recuperating from lung cancer surgery; he'd had half of his left lung removed after forty years of smoking.

Just a month before, he'd flown in his Beechcraft Bonaza up to the Bay Area for a visit. The plane's number read N41RA. Dad's first name is Ira. As I waited on the tarmac, he jumped lightly down the plane's stairs, wearing his old black leather flight jacket that had about a dozen patches from air shows. Shoved up on his head were the headphones he used to talk to the tower. He carried a piss pot, which he handed to me to hold.

Now when I walked into his room, Dad lay in bed in a light-blue hospital robe, his bare legs sticking out. A respirator was taped to his face, a heart monitor beeped away near the bed, and the TV was

on. His reading glasses; *Space*, by James Michener; and the Airline
Owners & Pilots Association magazine, *Pilot*, lay on a side table.
Despite his pallor, he looked strong. My mother was asleep in an
armchair next to the window, but lifted her head and smiled when I
came in. Her face was drawn, her hair looked like it needed a wash
and setting. I could feel the tension in her body when she got up
and gave me a long bear hug. Tears started to roll down her ashen
checks. I choked up, but through an effort of will managed not to
cry. I couldn't remember the last time I'd cried. It was probably
around the time Glenn beat me up for burying his coveted match-
box racing cars in the sandbox.

"Tell me how the meeting went, Son," Dad said. He'd pushed
a button, and the head of the bed rose until he was semisitting.

"It went okay," I said quietly. "At least I got my freedom." I felt
bad that I had to separate from the council, but believed I had no
choice.

"That's great son. Now you can go out and make a buck.
What's your plan?"

I told him I'd been thinking of starting my own green consulting company. That was the best I could come up with, to stay in
green building and be independent. I'd had enough of working
for anybody else, though; it just wasn't in my blood.

"Well, I wish you well with it," Dad said. "You know consulting
provided a wonderful life for me." He stopped and took a deep
breath. "But it's important for you to follow your heart." A warm,
peaceful feeling surged through me; that was the first time I'd
ever heard that from him.

"How are *you*?" I asked.

"I won't be climbing Everest anytime soon, but they think they
got all the cancer out. How are you two doing?" Dad asked Mom
and me.

"Not so great," I said. "I'm scared." I reached out to grab his hand.

"I don't want you to worry. No matter what happens, I've lived a full life. I have no regrets." More tears started to stream down Mom's face. I wished I could cry too. "I want you to take care of your mother."

But Dad didn't die. Like an old bull, he grew stronger. Eventually he asked me to fax his clean bill of health to the Federal Aviation Administration so he could get back the pilot's license they'd suspended when he'd been diagnosed.

CHAPTER 10

On My Own Again

WHEN I ARRIVED back in San Francisco, I closed the council office. I would work from home—if I found work to do. Each morning I got up and went out for a muffin and coffee on Chestnut Street. I found it hard to walk the block back home and get to work. I had no clients, no projects, and no income.

I worked the phones for a few months, calling just about everyone I knew in green building to see if they had any consulting work for me. Then one day I got a return call from Annette Osso at Public Technology, the nonprofit arm for the League of Cities, a membership organization comprising hundreds of local governments. Annette managed the environmental program and wanted my help producing a process-oriented book on how to make a green building, to be called *The Sustainable Building Technical Manual*. In addition, she wanted the council to serve as a peer review entity and to lend its name to the book. The lead funding source was the U.S. Environmental Protection Agency, with additional funds contributed by the Department of Energy.

And so I landed my first client. I'd be the managing editor for the book and contribute some chapters. My first tasks were to arrange the council's peer review and endorsement with the new D.C. association manager, Tom Cohn, and bring in Lynn Simon, now also an independent consultant, as my project manager. More hands-on than I, she knew the content experts we needed to round up in each of the sixteen areas of green building we identified. When it was finished, the Manual filled a void, defining the components and process for creating a green building, as we had tried to do in our stalled ASTM standard. It also provided a checklist of recommended strategies and resources, and a few case studies. The book later became a standard for the new industry, going through several rounds of publication.

Then in late 1994, the project of my dreams fell into my lap. I'd been invited to a cocktail party in San Francisco, a gathering of Public Technology's West Coast members hosted by Annette. A heavyset fellow in his late fifties sat down next to me. I introduced myself, and he said his name was Rich Hays and that he was director of the Department of the Environment for the City of San Diego.

"What do you do?" he asked.

"I'm a green building consultant."

"Really! That's a coincidence. I just bought a building for my department and we want to green it."

"Tell me about the building," I said, almost licking my lips in anticipation.

"We bought a vacant building in the Kearny Mesa area of the city. It's about 75,000 square feet and needs a full renovation." He paused. "We've just brought on an architect and some engineers. Green was part of their contract, but tell me how you can help us?"

A week later I flew to San Diego at Rich's invitation. I was so excited and nervous that I hadn't been able to sleep the night before. I needed this project, but didn't know what to expect, having never done a green building project from start to finish before.

As a developer, especially in the early years when I lacked experience, I'd succeeded by identifying and diligently managing the best technical professionals. I hoped I could do the same here.

Chuck Angyal picked me up at the airport. As chief architect and head of new-construction energy-efficiency programs at San Diego Gas and Electric, he would, I knew, be a valuable resource for the project. About ten years older than me and balding, Chuck wore a flowery tie, the kind an architect would wear. I was glad I'd worn a tie myself. Since leaving D.C. I'd avoided them, unless I was meeting a client or joining my parents at temple for the high holidays. Now, though, the city was a potential client, so a tie felt right.

As we walked to the car, we had a lot to talk about. In discussing the Department of the Environment building project the previous week by phone, Chuck had raised an interesting possibility. He told me that SDG&E had wanted to build an energy demonstration center (Southern California Edison, Southern California Gas, and Pacific Gas and Electric all had one), but the utility public-good funds within the state had dried up for such projects. Now, Chuck thought, we might be able to make this building into a mini–energy center, complete with displays and a tour.

We drove north on the freeway to the tired-looking brick-faced building, which was located at the end of Ridgehaven Court on a hill overlooking Interstate 15. About fifteen years old, it had been vacant since the tenant, General Dynamics, moved out several years before. The building had an east-west exposure, receiving San Diego's strong morning and evening sunlight through its long rows of tall ribbon windows. It had two mirror wings connected by a common lobby on each of its three floors, all of which needed some sprucing up. I'd read the engineering inspection report on the plane and knew that all of the systems required replacement: mechanical, electrical, plumbing, fire, and life safety. The city had paid $3 million for the property, totaling only $40 per square foot. That seemed like a good deal to me. However, their $20-per-square-foot budget for the full building renovation was too low. I'd mentioned that to Rich when we last talked on the phone. He said he had other resources if necessary. His department ran the Miramar landfill and collected the waste disposal fees. That gave them a separate source of revenue, as opposed to other agencies that relied solely on the city's general fund. He then told me about the project's tight schedule. The department was leasing space with a termination date less than a year away. The lease called for double rent thereafter.

Chuck and I met Rich and his project manager, Adam Saling, at a construction table set up on the building's first floor. The ceiling tile had already been removed, as had the carpeting, doors, and most of the walls. Rich and Chuck hit it off; they immediately started brainstorming about creating the best green building in the city, a showcase project for the city and the utility. A jolt of energy pulsed through me as I imagined hundreds of people touring the building to learn about the green features I'd helped specify and install. "Did you recycle the demolition debris?" I asked.

"Of course," Adam said. "We're salvaging and recycling almost all of the materials that come out of the building." As the environmental services department, waste reduction was one of their mandates.

Later that morning I met the project architect, Alison Whitelaw, as we toured the building along with several other members of the design team. "I've heard a lot about your work at the council," she said to me in a British accent. Wearing a long white dress with a flowing Hermès scarf and pearl necklace and earrings, she looked dressed for afternoon tea. Her firm had won the city's bidding competition to become the architect of record for the project. I had worried that, given my late arrival, the project design team would be hostile, since they were fairly far along with the plans, but I needn't have been concerned.

I walked into the first floor men's room. It would need a full renovation—new tile, floor, fixtures, toilets, paint. It smelled from lack of ventilation, making my stay brief. Next we took the elevator to the top floor. It worked fine, and they planned to keep it intact. The main office space on both sides of the elevator lobby had lots of windows. I breathed a little easier seeing the high level of sunlight penetration into the core of the space. Heat gain through the untinted, single-pane windows would, I imagined, be something of a problem, with the afternoon sun beating on the western façade. Adam later confirmed that the southwest corner offices were more like greenhouses than office space.

I followed the team up the metal ladder to the roof. It was black, with patches everywhere, and needed replacement, as did the old cooling towers, boilers, fans, and motors. "Are you thinking about installing a cool roof and a high level of insulation?" I asked Alison. A cool, or light-colored, roof would incur less heat gain from the sun, which in conjunction with more insulation would mean a lower air conditioning requirement on the top floor.

"That's a good idea," she said. "We hadn't thought about the impact of the roof's color yet."

We clambered back down the ladder to the third floor. "What about the mechanical heat pumps?" I asked, looking up at the inefficient old boxed units mounted to the ceiling.

"We'll buy all new heat pumps but keep the ducting," said Mitch, the mechanical engineer. I had contacts through the council with several of the major manufacturers of heat pumps and thought that I could help out with their specification and purchase. I made a mental note to add procurement assistance to the consulting services I'd pitch later in the day to Rich and Chuck.

"What are your thoughts on lighting?" I asked, surveying the old T-12 two-by-four-foot fluorescent fixtures stacked on the floor. I was told that they would be recycled for scrap metal and glass. When I mentioned the new daylighting sensors that dimmed the lights to Pervez, the electrical engineer, he was enthusiastic.

After the tour, we assembled around the makeshift tables on the first floor. Alison said that the construction drawings were already 75 percent complete. My stomach muscles clenched. That wasn't so great. Rich saw my concern and asked what I was thinking. I told everyone that I thought the building was ideal for a green demonstration project, but that if I came on board the schedule would be set back two months. To my relief, all parties agreed easily to this. Chuck then said that if the building achieved a high level of energy efficiency, with displays installed on the first floor, his utility would pay my bill and even finance the energy upgrades. Rich grinned at this news. It was all I could do to keep myself from jumping up and down.

After the meeting, Rich and Chuck asked me to put together a consulting proposal to make the building into the leading green building demonstration project in the state. "No problem," I said. "I can get it to you next week." I didn't have a clue how to do that.

That night after flying home and climbing into bed, I pulled out *The Earth Summit Strategy to Save Our Planet*, the book summarizing the agreements (known as Agenda 21) made at the 1992

Rio de Janeiro Earth Summit. In the introduction, editor Daniel Sitarz writes: "As humanity approaches the end of the century, it is poised at a crossroads of unmatched magnitude. The very existence of human life on Earth may well depend upon the direction which is taken in the next few years." I looked up and thought, "At least I'm doing my best." We'd make the building green, and we'd cut energy use by at least 50 percent.

I had never bid a project as a green building consultant or hired a green team of outside subcontractors. Although we'd done some energy efficiency work at my cousins' firm, that was much more limited. I called my dad for help, hoping to benefit from his thirty years of consulting experience. He gave me an hour crash course that proved invaluable: helping me figure out a scope of work, who to hire for help, deliverables, pricing and a schedule for our services.

Somehow, despite my doubts, I managed to put together a consulting plan. It called for two brainstorming rounds with the full team; several iterations of energy modeling; life-cycle costing of the energy package; procurement of green items as cheaply as possible (for this I invented the City of San Diego Ridgehaven Building Industry Partners Program); utilization of the utility's custom finance program; ongoing review of the project's plans and specifications; a commissioning review of the finished construction work; and drafting of a green operations manual and a case study at the end of the project.

I identified a good team for the energy component of my consulting work: Clark Bisel at Flack & Kurtz Engineers, and Steve Taylor, who would do the energy modeling and building commissioning. I tacked on the markups as dad suggested and sent off my proposal: $110,000. It seemed like a huge amount to me. If it was accepted, I'd finally be making some money. Even more important, I would have landed my first real green building project.

Chuck called the next week to tell me that the contract had been approved. His firm would split the cost with their membership association, EPRI (Electric Power Research Institute). I was on my way. I'm embarrassed to admit that as a reward I actually went out and leased a brand-new Jeep Grand Cherokee. I was doing a lot of fishing in northern California, and the Jeep off-road package included higher ground clearance and metal plates under the gas tank. I tried to ignore its listed gas consumption: 18 MPG on the highway, and even worse in the city.

Although in future project proposals I would also include the cost of getting technical advice in the selection of green building materials, Alison had already hired Lynn Froeschle for this purpose. A sufferer from multiple chemical sensitivity (MCS), Lynn was allergic to most traditional building products—adhesives such as carpet glue, the binders used in cabinet substrates, and finishes like paint and varnish. Her charge on the project was to find products that not only were attractive but also had limited toxicity and low volatile organic compound (VOC) emission levels.

At our meeting, Chuck's firm had set a target level for energy consumption of 9 kilowatt hours (KWh) per square foot. I didn't even know if that was possible under the best of circumstances, much less given the city's limited budget and a tight schedule. General Dynamics, the last tenant, had operated at an average of 21 KWh per square foot. That meant I had to come up with a 60 *percent* reduction over previous actual use. I'd asked Clark Bisel what the energy requirements would be under California's Title 24 energy code. He passed the question on to Steve Taylor, who did some analytic energy modeling and came up with 18 KWh per square foot—still making our goal of 9 KWh a 50 percent reduction relative to the legal standard.

As a result of our two brainstorming sessions held in early 1995, we decided to buy new high-efficiency water-source heat pumps, thereby raising efficiency by about 40 percent. We'd install a comprehensive lighting system with both direct (downward-pointing) and indirect (bouncing light off the ceiling) fixtures, using only one light tube (instead of four), an efficient electronic ballast, and both occupancy and daylight sensors. Our lighting goal was 0.73 watt per square foot, over 50 percent less than code. Most of the day, the lights would be powered down, since the extensive daylight would provide plenty of illumination. Clark suggested that we install and link the occupancy sensors with the mechanical system in all large rooms, since unoccupied space does not require lighting or temperature conditioning. Due to San Diego's mild year-round climate, it wasn't necessary to replace the windows with superefficient double-paned windows. Instead we decided to install a solar film made by Llumar on the windows. We'd replace the two rooftop cooling towers with new ones with variable-frequency drives for added control and efficiency. The employee workstations would have adjustable and energy-efficient fluorescent task lights and smart power-surge strips, also with occupancy sensors. Because a good deal of the city's computer equipment was too old to meet the EPA's new Energy Star guidelines, the sensors would help with the old monitors. Any new purchases would be Energy Star compliant. We also set a policy that employees could not install their own space heaters, which consume a lot of power. In any case, if the new heat pumps worked as designed, space heaters wouldn't be necessary.

Efficient lights, window film, and new equipment would lower the building's heat gain, allowing a reduction in the load requirements of the heat pumps. That translated into savings of over $100,000. We also saved money when we downsized the lighting fixtures to single tubes. Taking advantage of the ample daylight streaming in the windows eliminated a quarter of the fixtures.

Next we turned our attention to water use. Our water goal was a 30 percent reduction from the code requirement. We started by installing efficient fixtures in all bathrooms and a waterless urinal in the first floor men's room. Waterless urinals save about 45,000 gallons each per year. Although they use no water, they are reliable and clean. Outside, a mix of indigenous and desert plants meant the landscaping would require minimal watering. We discussed installing a cistern to capture rainwater off the roof, but San Diego's annual rainfall is so low that we couldn't justify the expense. We also talked about installing a dual-plumbing graywater system to capture sink water, but decided against this too. We didn't need recycled water for our landscaping, and it would be too expensive to filter it for reuse in the building.

Waste reduction was next. This was an important goal for the building, especially since Rich's department was responsible for both recycling and waste minimization within the city. They'd already salvaged a lot of the original tenant improvements, and the low-bid contractor would be charged with doing the same. Later, a case study was published showing that the project had diverted over 50 percent of its waste from the landfill—186 tons of construction debris, for a total cost savings of $93,000. This was a high level at the time, though not many years later it would be considered the minimum, as leading projects in the state began hitting savings figures of over 90 percent. After the building was completed, ongoing recycling would remain a high priority. For this purpose we included numerous recycling areas and a collection system in the design.

Lynn chose products with high recycled content—ceiling tile, drywall, insulation, ceramic bathroom tile, toilet partitions, fiberboard—and products that were themselves recyclable—carpet tiles, walls built for disassembly, movable workstations. When it came to paints, glues, fiberboard, wood finishes, and cleaning materials, she found products that promoted good air quality. We also specified dual air filters and flushing out the building with 100 percent outside air for two weeks after construction to get rid of pollutants resulting from any off-gassing of materials and finishes. Some of the doors and other items would be spray painted off-site to further lessen contamination of the building itself.

Steve ran a new building energy analysis after we'd finalized all of our selections. We found that the overall energy consumption projection had fallen to 8.3 KWh per square foot. We'd beat the goal!

Now we had to figure out how to get the money for all this. The total project construction cost was just over $3 million, plus the previous purchase of the building at another $3 million. The largest budget item was the new HVAC and electrical systems— 27 percent of the total cost. Clark and Steve had calculated that the incremental add-on for the higher-level energy items (relative to conventional systems) would cost about $270,000, though they'd pay for themselves in less than three years. The problem was that the city didn't have the funds for the measures we were proposing (a common problem, I later learned). As a result, it was necessary to come up with an alternative method of financing and procurement, something that I later named "green finance."

In the realm of energy, we got lucky; SDG&E agreed to finance $230,000 of the $270,000, with a loan that the city would pay back over five years through the savings from the building's monthly energy bill. The remaining $40,000 would be paid by the city.We projected a high rate of return on that relatively minor net investment.

We still had to solve the problem of higher-priced green materials, and for this we created the City of San Diego Ridgehaven Building Industry Partners Program. We convinced the city attorney to let us sole-source products that had unique environmental performance—meaning, we could purchase directly from individual manufacturers who specialized in certain green product lines. Lynn Froeschle selected the qualifying materials—paint, insulation, floor tile, ceiling tile—while Clark and the project engineers came up with the energy items, such as lighting, sensors, heat pumps, and window film. In return for publicity that included signage in the building and being showcased in a display, we asked that the sole-sourced manufacturers knock 25 percent off their normal "market" price.

I was in charge of designing this program and getting the manufacturers to go for it. To my delight, the task proved relatively easy, and we soon had eight firms signed up. By going straight to the manufacturer, we cut out four levels of markups (the usual supply chain for our industry being from manufacturer to distributor to supplier to subcontractor to contractor to owner), saving about $130,000. This approach also allowed us to skip the public bid process that allows contactors to include "or equal" substitutions in their bid.

The city didn't have the money for carpet tile, which is more costly than broadloom carpet. Carpet tile, however, has numerous environmental advantages over traditional carpeting. For one thing, it lasts longer and, because it comes in individual eighteen-by-eighteen-inch squares (as opposed to the twelve-foot-long sections of broadloom), is much less wasteful to replace if it is damaged. It often includes recycled content from old carpet, and is itself recyclable. Finally, installation is easy and requires very little low VOC adhesive (if any). In the end, we arranged to sole-source Interface's carpet tile (13 percent postindustrial recycled content) through their five-year Evergreen carpet leasing program—the second building in the country to participate in this innovative plan. The city was happy to divert the $130,000 initial payment, and savings from our energy-efficient design would easily offset the monthly lease payment. Private companies gain an added advantage from such a leasing program, since they can write off the lease payment each year, as opposed to having to amortize the carpet over a longer period. Such an arrangement can work for all types of building products and systems, yet it is rarely undertaken in the building industry.

After we'd finished the plans and specifications, the green renovation project went out to public bid. Alison and her team had written green guidelines for the contractor's waste recycling and salvaging, indoor air quality during construction, and other measures. Unfortunately, the city is required to accept the low bidder, whatever their qualifications in green building. (In 1999, I was glad to help the State change this process, allocating a significant percentage of the selection evaluation points for "green.")

Some years later, in 2002, I took a tour of the building with Ken Jordan, the engineer selected by the city to monitor the building control system and make sure it worked as designed. The Interface carpet tiles still looked good, as did the environmental paint from AFM and the ceiling tiles from Eurostone (no

man-made fibers, formaldehyde binders, or organic materials).
The lighting system from Genlyte/Lightolier was still considered
cutting edge, seven years later. Computer screen glare was minimal due to the bounced light from the ceiling-mounted fixtures.
The occupancy sensor went into action when I entered one of
the conference rooms, turning on the lights and air conditioning.
It would turn them off again when the room was empty for a pre-
determined period.

After reviewing the six years of operating data that Ken provided, I was ecstatic to see that the building had averaged 8.3
KWh per square foot in energy consumption (the same number
Steve Taylor had projected in 1996). During the energy crisis in
2000, when the city's utility rates more than doubled, the building
virtually coined money for the city, and it is still saving about
$80,000 in energy costs every year. That's about $1.10 per square
foot of space. Ultimately, the city achieved a 57 percent internal
rate of return on its $40,000 investment. I imagine this was one of
their better investments.

Ken told me that city employees have loved the building. At
one point, the city shifted employees who complained about poor
air quality in other city buildings into Ridgehaven, and the complaints faded away.

Behind Ridgehaven is a mirror-image sister building occupied
by the Sheriff's Department. For five years after we finished
Ridgehaven, it was the same on the surface, but without our
green elements—and we used the energy consumption in that
building as a baseline to gauge our building's performance.
Whereas we had cut our utility costs by more than half, they continued paying the full bill. A few years ago, they'd had enough of
our showing them up and renovated the building, incorporating
many of our green features.

According to the city, the new building's water-efficient appliances and landscaping save approximately 500,000 gallons of water each year, 45 percent more than before. The reduced electricity consumption has lowered CO_2 emissions by about 500 tons annually, SO_2 by 1.4 tons, and NO_x by 1.3 tons.

As a demonstration project, thousands of enthusiasts from more than forty-five countries have visited Ridgehaven. Other San Diego city buildings went green, and in 1997 the mayor passed a green building ordinance. The city later adopted the U.S. Green Building Council's green building rating system. We'd proved that green building could be achieved even with the constraints of a city budget, a tight schedule, and city low-bidder procurement laws.

As Ken and I walked through the lobby, I spotted a thirty-foot cabinet filled to bursting with environmental awards and trophies the building had won. Among them was the U.S. Department of Energy and Environmental Protection Agency's Energy Star Building Label: Ridgehaven was the first building in the country to receive that coveted award. It also won the governor's environmental award for California, the U.S. Navy's Commander's Award, and dozens of others.

Ridgehaven taught me that finishing a successful green building is like competing in an Ironman triathlon. After the open-ocean 2.4-mile swim, you have a 112-mile bike ride, and then you finish with a full marathon. The goal is not merely to participate in the race, but to cross the finish line. With Ridgehaven, as with most projects I later learned, we moved two steps forward and one step back throughout the project. Money was always an issue. At one point Rich went to the city council for more money and was turned down; even Mayor Susan Golding voted against us. We did get the money later, with the help of SDG&E—and even later, not surprisingly, the mayor and the city council had no qualms about accepting the Energy Star Building Award at a closed-session meeting.

In December 1995 I walked into San Francisco's renowned Shreve & Co. jewelry store on Post Street, my credit cards burning a hole in my pocket. I'd grossed $250,000 in my first year of consulting. Green building was a real business, and the number of pioneers undertaking green projects was increasing.

"Can I help you?" the graying, slightly stooped saleswoman asked me.

"I'd like to try on the silver Rolex—the Explorer II." I felt an urge to look around and make sure nobody I knew was watching. She opened the display cabinet and handed me the watch. A big black face filled the thick stainless-steel casing, Rolex's signature raised date magnifier giving it added distinction. I was surprised at how heavy it was. I'd always wanted a Rolex. I thought about the gold Cartier my cousins had bought me; I hadn't worn it since leaving D.C. But this was different, I told myself. This I'd earned on my own. Besides, it was waterproof to 330 feet and rugged enough to withstand a nuclear blast; it would last a lifetime—and that was green, wasn't it? "I'll take it," I said, pulling out my platinum American Express credit card, the same card Jim had. $3,500!

"Wear it in good health," my dad said that evening when I called to tell my parents about my purchase. "You're on your way," he added. "I did the same thing after my first million-dollar year of consulting. You've seen my gold Patek Philipe?" I looked at my wrist. I was really on my way again!

"Mazel Tov. I'm so proud of you," Mom added. "Maybe now you can take a break. You looked so tired during your last visit."

My next project, in 1995, was among the first demonstration green buildings for the U.S. Navy, its Building 33 in southwest Washington, D.C., along the waterfront. I assembled a small green team that helped me advise the designers on energy systems and green building materials. The former gun turret plant was being renovated into a 150,000-square-foot four-story office building. It turned out to be another award-winning green building, with a high level of performance — 30 percent below a conventionally renovated building, with $135,000 a year in energy savings. The payback period for the incremental energy investment was less than one year. Its features included Heat Mirror high-efficiency glazing, insulation with an R-value of 30, light sensors, and low-VOC building finishes. The building's energy-efficient design provided for a reduction in the conventional HVAC system by 36 percent, resulting in $200,000 of first-cost savings. Afterward, an order stipulated that all future Navy construction projects be green as well.

Next was the conversion of Kansas City's 1914 Union Station into a science museum, restoring the structure back to its original glory. My client was Kansas City Power and Light, which tried to copy my arrangement with San Diego Gas and Electric on the Ridgehaven project. They paid my fee and then donated my services to the museum's development and design team as a customer benefit. The utility also wanted to make the million-square-foot building into a showcase for renewable energy and other state-of-the-art energy systems. However, in contrast to the Ridgehaven situation, where the city was a determined advocate, in this case the owner and developer weren't able to embrace green building. The project was strictly cost and schedule driven. I'd led a green brainstorming session for the entire team, but few of my green team's suggestions were adopted. It was a frustrating experience after the success of Ridgehaven, especially given the incredible opportunity that the building's history and intended use offered.

In late 1996 a woman named Kath Williams approached me at the annual USGBC conference, held that year in San Diego. "I want to know everything you know about green building," she said. "We're going to set the standard for university green building." Kath, it turned out, was the project manager for a new campus laboratory building (later named the EpiCenter Building) to be built at Montana State University. She told me that she was finishing up a Ph.D. in education at MSU and had also taught at Stanford. As tall as I was, and probably stronger, she had a deep, bold voice, thick glasses, and curly brown hair. I got the impression that whatever she wanted, she got. She had heard my keynote address at the conference, had toured Ridgehaven, and now was interested in having me fly out to meet the top brass of the university. I already knew something about the project, since MSU was one of the five NIST grantees for the congressional green building demonstration program several years earlier. They had gone on to receive several rounds of additional funding from Congress.

The next month I arrived in freezing Bozeman. I joined Bob Berkebile, the lead architect for the new building. A broad-based team had already been assembled for the project—one that included many of my colleagues from the council—and several design charettes (intensive and integrated team brainstorms) had been conducted over the previous two years.

I was delighted to have the opportunity to work with Bob. His team's vision for the project was decidedly forward-looking: fuel cells that ran off hydrogen generated by a solar-powered water splitting machine, solar algae ponds to treat wastewater from the lab on-site, unprecedented levels of daylighting, locally sourced materials, low-energy fume hoods for the labs, wireless equipment, an enormous vision wall for students to observe ongoing lab experiments, and dozens of other innovations. The team wanted this to be the global model for campus green building.

I worked for MSU over the next two years, and helped put together an industry partnership program that was adopted by the state. But the project soon ran into problems. As the team's wish list grew ever longer, the budget fattened—from $11 million to $90 million at one point. The university simply didn't have the name, infrastructure, or experience to raise that much money. Meanwhile, the only new funding that had come in was a multimillion-dollar technology innovation grant, given by Congress as the last installment in the demonstration program funding. All of us consultants were paid out of the congressional funds when the university flew us in for a dozen or more meetings. Much of the rest of the money was spent on mapping local materials resources, developing the technology for the low-energy fume hood, and the closed-loop energy system for converting water into hydrogen fuel—fantastic ideas, but probably not the best use of the limited project budget.

In the meantime, I did the work I'd been hired to do: bringing thirty companies to the university to partner at a 25 percent product-cost discount, and working with Kath to get the industry partnership program that I'd drafted passed by the governor. But I couldn't help make the project happen. Due to financing problems, it was clear that my work was fruitless, and that didn't feel right. As a team we'd done what my dad always advised against: confused efforts with results.

During the first year of my work with MSU, I was caught up in the general excitement. Although I worried about where the money was going to come from, I hoped for the best. Eventually, though, I felt compelled to voice my worries to Kath's boss, Tom McCoy, vice president of research. In October 1998, well into my second year on the project, we were walking down the hall in the administration building and he'd asked me how things were going.

"Not that well," I said quietly. Before I knew it, he was steering me into his office. "I'm in conference," he shouted to his secretary as he shut the door. He told me that he too was worried. I felt like I was letting the team down, but I also realized I had a fiduciary responsibility. "You're paid to do a job," my father had said to me one evening on the phone. "If something is preventing you from performing, you need to alert the client."

I suggested to McCoy that the university either delay the project in order to raise money, or scale down the plan.

Shortly afterward, Tom put the project on hold. To date it hasn't been built. The university's allocated project funds were used in renovation of its main library, the student union, and a portion was returned to the university's general fund. The team's inventions were published in a NIST report with CD-ROM, so others can benefit from the hard work and creativity of the team. Some of the prototyped technologies are still operating as MSU's nearby technology office park. However, the green passion remained, as faculty members developed new green research projects and several students graduated and formed a construction waste management company. Kath finished her Ph.D. at the university and went on to open her own green building consulting firm. Just after we started working together she joined the USGBC board of directors as our university representative. Her strong take-charge approach and people skills led her to become one of our two vice chairs, a position she still holds. She has retained her passion for green building and helped coach the council's educational programs, a focus of her new company. And the rest of us went on to do more projects, using many of the innovations we arrived at through our creative brainstorming and extensive technical research for MSU.

The MSU project made me think hard about my role as a consultant. What do I do if I'm being well compensated but know the project is unlikely to succeed? When is it time to quit? Even now, after almost a decade, I am still trying to feel my way on these questions. The Montana experience taught me many lessons. For one thing, it is critical that the project start with a deep commitment at the top of the organization, as we'd had with Rich Hays at Ridgehaven.

In September 1997 I visited my parents for Rosh Hashanah services at University Synagogue in Los Angeles. I go home for one of the two Jewish high holidays each year. I'm not much for temple—I get more meaning hiking in nature—but I do it to honor my parents, listen to the beautiful voice of the cantor, and say hello to some old friends.

The next day I went over to pitch new consulting work to the City of Santa Monica. The year before, I'd put in a bid to the city to develop green building guidelines, but lost to a lower bidder. Still, that bidding process had allowed me to become friendly with Susan Munves, the city's environmental manager. Her office was on the Santa Monica Pier, where I'd learned to fish at twelve, riding my bike from our house in the hills near Mount Saint Mary's College, just behind the new Getty Museum.

Susan and I eventually did start working together, after I'd dreamed up a new program called BuildingFutures, based on the Ridgehaven success. Its focus was on optimizing the development process in five steps: (1) project definition and management, (2) identification of best-practice design areas, (3) life cycle investment, (4) building performance assurance, and (5) communication of results. The main feature was BuildingCamp, a highly interactive brainstorm session. It was my version of the green charettes that projects now included, but it was driven by results, not process. Susan wanted me to do a BuildingCamp for Santa Monica's new $30 million public safety facility. The project was just getting under way, and the city wanted to showcase its new green building guidelines.

The site was tightly sandwiched between City Hall and the Santa Monica Freeway. It was hard for me to imagine a multistory 150,000-square-foot building and parking deck going up here, but that was the plan. The new complex would house the city's police, fire, and public safety departments, as well as a jail, shooting range, cafeteria, and offices.

Susan had arranged for me to meet her boss, Craig Perkins, head of Public Works, to discuss the project. The morning of our meeting was just perfect: The sun was shining brightly, and there was a fresh ocean breeze. As I walked along Palisades Park, a grassy stretch studded with huge palm trees, I was transported back to my childhood and the picnics my family used to have there. In those days, one could hear Yiddish, Russian, and Hebrew all along the greensward.

When I arrived at Craig's office, Susan was sitting at his conference room table with a cup of coffee, and Craig was on the phone at his desk. He was slender and fit, his wiry energy making him pace back and forth during the call. "Tell him I want it done by tomorrow," he said to the party on the phone. "He's had enough time." Craig hung up, but before I could say hello, his secretary bolted in to give him his messages. "Tell George I can't meet this afternoon. I'm in hearings."

Finally he turned to me. "How can you help us with our project?"

Great. There was a fish there, but how was I going to land it? "Go steady, David," I told myself, then launched into my sales pitch, outlining the services I'd developed for BuildingFutures. I handed Craig a copy of the booklet, hot off the presses, explaining the program. The cover resembled a blueprint, light blue with a thin line drawing showing the C. K. Choi Building at the University of British Columbia, solar panels perched on the roof (something I still hoped to see installed in one of my projects). Craig flipped through the booklet, nodding his head. Then he went to the white board and began scribbling categories for the environmental goals of the new public safety building: energy, water, and waste. "What levels do you suggest?" he asked.

"A 50 percent reduction for energy, 30 for water, and 75 percent waste diversion," I said.

The meeting was relatively brief but dense. Craig asked good questions, and my answers apparently satisfied him because I went home with a new client. He'd bought the full menu of services, including my first BuildingCamp.

On this job I needed even more outside expert help than I had at Ridgehaven. I retained Anthony Bernheim, an architect with SMWM Architects, whose San Francisco Public Library project had been a pioneer in green building, featuring incredible daylighting and indoor air quality. I also retained Malcolm Lewis, president of Constructive Technologies Group, to do energy modeling, indoor air and systems analysis, and peer review of the drawings.

I opened a new office in downtown San Francisco on New Montgomery, right at Mission, a small tenth-floor suite with a view of the bay. I installed Interface carpet tiles, AFM paint, and efficient lights with sensors. More projects came in: the Marin Community Foundation, Starbucks, a project for Kent Swig, and DreamWorks. I hired staff to help out. On one sunny Saturday, I even leased a new sky-blue BMW Z3 convertible, rationalizing that it was more "eco" than my Jeep, given that it had less embodied energy with only two seats and a tiny trunk that couldn't fit my golf clubs. A few years later, my conscience led me to end my lease early and take delivery of the newly introduced Toyota Prius hybrid car that got forty-five miles per gallon. It was a hard but necessary transition: "eco" for speed.

CHAPTER 11

My Dinner with Rick

THE ASSOCIATION management company that Mike had brought in to take my place didn't work out. Members were not renewing, complaints were rising. We hired Bostrom Corporation in their place, a larger, more established association management firm in downtown D.C. They assigned us a staff executive director who managed three other nonprofits. I told myself it would work out this time. A few months passed as I continued building my consulting business.

"Can you meet me in L.A. for dinner next week?" It was April 1996, and Rick Fedrizzi was on the phone. He was flying out for a Carrier meeting from his base in Syracuse.

"What's up?"

"I'll tell you when we get together." I wondered what he wanted to talk about. Something in his tone alerted me that this was not going to be a purely social dinner. Was it his job at Carrier, or his family? The council?

At seven sharp I walked into the Ivy, located on the beach in Santa Monica. As I waited for Rick in the entry area, watching the hustle and bustle of the groovy patrons and fast-moving staff at the lively restaurant he'd selected, I realized it felt good to sit down. I'd been out late the night before with my brothers, celebrating

Glenn's birthday. It was rare for the three of us to get together without our parents and my brothers' families, and we'd managed to
while away many hours simply enjoying one another's company.

When Rick came into the restaurant, I sat up in my seat,
shocked. He'd been dieting and looked emaciated: His cheekbones jutted out in sharp relief, and his pants looked as if they'd
fall down if it weren't for his belt. He was easily thirty pounds
lighter than when I'd last seen him several months before.
Spotting me, he grinned and came over to give me a bear hug.

We caught up over the meal. He was about to celebrate his
eighteenth wedding anniversary, and his two kids were growing
up fast. Even though we were only five years apart in age, I
reflected sadly that I had yet to begin that part of my life.

When they brought dessert and coffee, Rick leaned back in his
chair and looked away. "I'm going to tell you something you're
not going to want to hear," he said at length. "Don't get angry."

I put down my fork, a chunk of chocolate cake still clinging to
it. "I'm listening." I inhaled deeply and leaned forward. A waiter
hurried by with a loaded tray of clanking dishes.

"If you don't come back to run the council, we'll be bankrupt
in a month," Rick said.

Words of protest rushed to my lips, but I had promised to listen.
The spicy taste of tandoori chicken rose in my gullet.

"The management company is killing what you, Mike, and I
created."

"It's out of the question, Rick. The last round almost killed
me," I said.

"You can call the shots," Rick pleaded. "Just let me know what
you need and I'll make it happen."

"No," I said.

As we parted to go to our cars, Rick again said, touching me on the shoulder, "Think about it."

Later that night I got into bed at my parents' house in L.A. The ceiling of my old bedroom was still cottage cheese. Grandpa Izzy's vinyl sofa chair stood in the corner; it had cracks running all through it and was faded to a puke-red color. Mom would never give that old thing away. I finally fell asleep, and soon I was having a familiar nightmare. I was at the council board table in D.C. Our vice chairman was yelling at me, "I told you, you'll get paid when you get our policies and procedures manual in order, and your buddy Mike in line!"

Everyone else looked out for themselves. Why couldn't I? I was finally making money, and at what I wanted: greening buildings. Why did I need to do anything more for the council? Hadn't I done enough already? At 6 a.m. I finally gave up trying to sleep and went for a run around Mount Saint Mary's College. Then I showered and called Rick at his hotel along the beach in Santa Monica.

"I knew you couldn't say no," Rick said when I told him I'd accept.

"I'm going to keep my consulting business. The council will have to be a client of my company," I said.

"Whatever you want."

Over the next few months I moved quickly to stabilize the council. I assigned two of my staff members to it full-time and personally called all the members who hadn't renewed their annual dues (about 40 percent of our 125 members). I nominated board members to take on critical committee assignments: the building rating system we'd been developing, our upcoming annual conference, the jump-start of our state and local government committee. We hadn't selected a location for our annual conference, so I chose San Diego, given my connections with the city and SDG&E, and the Ridgehaven building as a place to tour. Since we were broke, Chuck got SDG&E to pay $15,000 in advance registration for fifty of his program's building owners to attend.

In mid-1996 I flew to Washington for a board meeting. The day before the meeting Mike and I met for dinner at Meskerem, my favorite Ethiopian restaurant, in Adams Morgan. Having settled on large pillows on the wood floor, we ordered a couple of Ethiopian beers. We'd share food from a large round plate, eating it with our hands, using flat injera bread to scoop up the spiced vegetables and tender beef and lamb. The weather was hot and humid, and we were both wearing shorts. Mike had on a patterned Hawaiian shirt, and I wore a golf shirt from Bajamar, a great course ninety minutes south of the border in Mexico. It was one of Chuck's favorites, and we'd played there a few times.

When our second round of beer arrived, I glanced over at Mike. "You need to let the pollution taxes effort go, Mike. It's not worth it."

He put his beer down. "Who got to you?"

"No one in particular. Everyone thinks the timing is still premature." Mike studied the colorful pattern of an adjacent pillow. I'd hurt my friend. "It's the wrong time. We've got to revive the council first." I listened to the melodic Ethiopian music on the loudspeaker for what seemed like an entire song.

"I understand," Mike said at last. He took a long pull from his bottle of beer. "I'll back off." I breathed a sigh of relief.

Rob Watson, our board member from NRDC, took over the leadership of the building rating system committee. In 1997 he'd arranged for an initial grant of $200,000 from the Department of Energy for a rating system pilot program; over the next two years, DOE added another $600,000. The committee gave the rating system the catchy name of LEED—Leadership in Energy and Environmental Design. It provided a point system that is sophisticated, yet easy to use. LEED quickly became both a powerful building design tool and a certification system for commercial new construction and major renovation. It is also fun for use in project greening brainstorming sessions, a game of sorts.

While using LEED to rate a prospective project, the goal is to earn the highest number of points in six defined environmental categories: Sustainable Sites (14 points possible), Water Efficiency (5 points), Energy and Atmosphere (17 points), Materials and Resources (13 points), Indoor Environment Quality (15 points), and Innovation and Design Process (5 points). There are four levels of awards distributed according to the number of LEED points earned by the project: Platinum—a minimum of 52 points (out of 69 total); Gold—39; Silver—33; and Certified—26.

Obtaining LEED certification requires registering a building project with the council and then, after the project is completed, submitting an application with supporting data to USGBC. It's a complicated and lengthy information-gathering and documentation process that the whole team helps with. Buildings are given a certificate and LEED plaque at the award level achieved, once approved by the council.

LEED provides the green building benchmarks, but doesn't tell applicants *how* to get the points; that's up to the team. For example, a building project can earn one point for using 20 percent less water than the minimum set by the Energy Policy Act of 1992, while a 30 percent reduction tacks on another point. Generating a minimum savings of 5 percent of energy through on-site renewable energy systems is worth one point, 10 percent adds another, and 30 percent yet another. The most cost-effective points are those for energy-efficient performance (receiving four to six of ten available points, the most of any credit category). Additional credits are earned for installing renewable energy into the project and developing a building monitoring and verification plan, including continuous equipment metering. Materials credits are achieved for reusing an existing building, managing construction waste, and specifying building materials that include recycled content or are local or rapidly renewable. Indoor environmental quality credits are earned for actions such as specifying low-emitting construction materials, providing for occupant thermal comfort, and maximizing daylight penetration into the building.

Soon after it was rolled out, LEED inspired a type of green building Olympics, with cities and private projects unofficially competing to see who could earn the highest LEED award. The federal government was one of the first to require its use for some of its leading agency projects. The Navy asks for a LEED Silver level, as does Seattle for civic buildings. Dozens of other cities have adopted the system, including New York, Los Angeles, San Diego, and Portland, Oregon. The council posted the LEED guidelines on its Web site so that the public could download it for free, and thousands of designers and building professionals are now actively using the system for their projects.

I began using LEED on all of my consulting projects, starting with Santa Monica's public safety facility. A few years later, I used it as a multiproject design tool for DeAnza Foothill District

Colleges. They'd hired me to help develop a sustainable design strategy for their two campuses with nine building projects being designed at the same time. In April 2001 we assembled one hundred professionals, representing all of the district's project design teams, as well as district staff and some students, in one large room at DeAnza College. Day one was dedicated to setting district-wide campus greening goals, while day two was entirely LEED focused.

On the second morning, the assembled teams brainstormed their way through LEED's credits in each category. I bounced from team table to team table. "Team One got six points for a 30 percent reduction in energy from code," I said to Team Three. "How come you guys are projecting a measly 10 percent reduction?" Team Three would then vow to beat Team One, redoubling its efforts.

Afterward, I reassembled the full group and had each team call out its LEED points in each of the six categories. The wildly different answers led to a dynamic competition that made everyone hot to beat the others. As I watched the participants (including the presidents of both colleges and the district chancellor) eagerly debating the merits of a higher energy efficiency level, on-site generation of renewable energy, and a higher level of waste diversion from the landfill, I felt overwhelmed with happiness. I recalled a meeting eight years earlier in the AIA boardroom, when as a younger man, I nervously presented my white paper on the need for a U.S. building rating system to sixty professionals.

LEED soon became the standard definition for a green building in the United States. It did what we'd hoped to do years before in the ASTM green building subcommittee. In two words, a concerned party could communicate a new building's or a city's green performance level, as Seattle's Mayor Paul Schell did in 1998 when he announced (at one of our board meetings hosted by the city in Seattle) his goal of "LEED Silver" for all new building projects in the city. The Hewlett Foundation earned LEED Gold in 2002 for their new headquarters in Menlo Park. I sat in the audience feeling like a doting grandparent as I watched the president of the foundation accept the award plaque from our president and CEO, Christine Ervin. She was called up to deliver remarks to the distinguished crowd, and then announced USGBC's first California LEED Gold award for the beautifully designed green building. In front of me sat Stanford's past president Gerard Casper and three members of the Hewlett family.

That all happened once the LEED program was well under way. The beginning of the process, however, required some fine-tuning. When the first few LEED applications were submitted to the council, we were shocked at their size: Each application write-up was a foot thick, bound in several large notebooks. Apparently, the LEED documentation requirements were burdensome, and led green building professionals to charge owners high fees for collecting, verifying, and organizing the data—a cost that naturally made building owners unhappy. The council took note, and the fees came down substantially with the release of version 2.1, which included time-saving standard templates in which the professionals could certify that the given LEED minimums had been met. Over the years, things became more streamlined, and eventually the council built up the LEED program into a full suite of products: a training course with approved faculty, a LEED reference guide, an extensive LEED Web site, and a LEED professional accreditation exam. Soon I began seeing "LEED AP" (Accredited Professional) on members' business cards, letterhead, and marketing materials. It made my heart swell with contentment. I then quickly began pushing the USGBC board to consider broadening the LEED accreditation exam and issuing the designation of "GBC" after one's name once they had passed the test and completed several years of green building.

By 2003, LEED had become the key to the greening of America's buildings. Its use had also spread overseas. Even private companies such as Ford, Toyota, Pottery Barn, Pier One, and PNC Bank used it. However, one of the greatest barriers to green building lay in obtaining accurate information on costs. In 2003 the council and a private consulting firm, Capital E, surveyed thirty-three green buildings and found the average cost increase for the LEED-certified buildings (certified through Platinum levels) was only 2 percent. Seattle and the state of Pennsylvania, where LEED Silver was required by law for public buildings, reported almost no cost increase as they gained increasing project-based LEED experience. The study showed that the cost of green has been coming down every year, falling 38 percent from 1995 to 2003.

Though most of the savings in green building come from improved energy and water efficiency, studies by Rocky Mountain Institute and Joseph Romm in his book _Lean and Clean Management_ found that in six green projects, employee productivity (including reductions in absenteeism) rose anywhere from 6 to 16 percent. Each year, employers pay more in salary than an entire building costs to construct. Over the course of thirty years for an owner-occupied building, Romm notes, only 3 percent of the total cost outlay is for the building's up-front design and construction, 6 percent goes for ongoing building operations, while 91 percent pays building-occupant employee salaries. A productivity increase of just 1 percent is double the savings of the entire annual energy bill; at 6 percent, the productivity savings is almost the same as an average rental payment. Employee productivity is the smoking gun of green building.

In the early years of green building, it was difficult to define and source out "sustainable products." LEED's credits helped here too. Soon, leading manufacturers were informing architects and building owners about their products' contributions to LEED credits. The council has always steered away from certifying products as "green," but LEED did provide a measure of guidance to the marketplace. Many of the council's manufacturer members have gone on to introduce sustainable products, including Armstrong, U.S. Gypsum, Interface, Milliken, Carrier, Herman Miller, and dozens of others. When Armstrong came out with a ceiling tile recycling program while working with one of our board members at Selen Construction (the project's construction manager), I felt like a proud parent. They had introduced a revolutionary product that would not only make the world a better place, but also save the client money.

LEED allowed me to lower my consulting fees. Before the program was instituted, I was often hired to *define* "green building" for a fee that could top $100,000. Afterward, I was hired to *implement* LEED. It took the mystery out of green building. Soon mainstream project managers and design teams will be thoroughly versed in LEED and green building, limiting the need for green building consultants. I consider this a sign of success.

In June 1996 I hired Kristin Ralff to help me run the council. She arrived for her interview sporting spiked hair, purple velvet skirt, black tights, and military boots. She bounced up and down in her chair and spoke so fast I had to shift my brain into high gear to keep up with her. She took to the council like a new mother bonds with her baby, and before long was managing the entire day-to-day operations. Her dress and grooming matured in parallel with her elevated responsibility. She was so good that my role quickly shifted to supervisory, with a set number of hours a month.

That year at the gala dinner of our conference in San Diego, as I took the podium, I spotted my parents in the tenth row. At the last minute, I'd asked them to the conference. I had never invited them to hear me speak, but I figured now was the right time.

My mom waved at me; I saw tears in her eyes. Dad smiled. He had a notepad in his lap and pen in hand. After my talk, my parents watched from a distance as people came up to talk with me. Mom was smiling broadly, while Dad stood reviewing his neatly outlined notes. I would later learn that I had too many uh's, not enough punch in delivery of key points, too many topics, not enough jokes, and only a medium-level crescendo at the closing. It took me years to understand that this was a form of love. He had recovered well from his lung surgery and a subsequent hip replacement, and now was back to golf and flying. "I'm proud of you, Son," he said, giving me a kiss on the cheek and a big hug. "We had no idea," Mom said, pointing at the room packed with hundreds of fellow green building advocates and council members.

My first public speech had been at my Bar Mitzvah in 1973, at University Synagogue on Sunset Boulevard in Brentwood. I'd written the talk on small note cards—and stood before my family and friends and nervously read each word. I somehow made it through the chanted Hebrew Torah portion, fearing every second that my voice would crack. "Speak loudly, clearly, and slowly," my dad had said.

Five years later I stood at a lectern in my high school's football stadium on a sunny day in early June addressing my nine hundred classmates and their families at our graduation in Pacific Palisades. I was senior class president. My hair was long and wavy—the brown curls just didn't brush down. This time, although I again copied the speech out on note cards, I delivered it from memory. I had practiced dozens of times in front of a mirror at home, with my parents coaching me.

When I first began to talk to audiences about green building, I was stiff. I stood awkwardly behind my slides and I would try to cover too much, leaving even the most sympathetic of audiences twitching in their seats.

In the summer of 1996, Ray Anderson, chairman of Interface carpet tile company and a man known as the "green CEO," put on a conference in San Francisco called "The Power of One." A hundred top building industry professionals and environmental leaders from around the Bay Area were there. He had asked seven environmentalists to speak; two of them were my idols. David Brower was the first executive director of the Sierra Club; had started four other environmental groups, including Friends of the Earth and Earth Island Institute; and had written four books. And Paul Hawken was the author of the bestseller *The Ecology of Commerce*, and now was working on *Natural Capitalism*. Visionary, concise, and able to speak the language of business and merge it with environmental needs, he is, for my money, the best speaker in the green movement.

But I wasn't there for the pleasure of hearing these towering figures speak. I was supposed to get up *on the same stage* with these guys!

I had only a month to prepare. When I asked our sponsor what I should talk about, Nanci Scoular of Interface froze my blood by saying, in her South African accent, *"Daaavid,* we want you to talk about yourself. What drives you? Why did you quit development and start the council?"

I'd never been asked to speak about myself before. No pictures of green buildings or PowerPoint slides to hide behind, no building case studies to present. Just me. I was terrified.

The night before the event, I filled a sheet of paper with crossed-out thoughts. What could I possibly have to say that these people would want to hear? Somehow, I wanted to talk about life, point out that it's short; tell them the planet is our only home, and we need to take care of it. It was nothing they hadn't heard before, but these were the ideas that stirred my soul.

The next morning, still not at all sure what I was going to say, I sat in the third row, mesmerized. "What we are all missing are operating instructions for the earth," David Brower was saying. "I propose CPR—Conservation, Preservation, and Restoration." At eighty-four, with a full head of gray hair and bushy eyebrows, he was the elder statesman of the environmental movement. In his prime, he had climbed the world's highest mountains alone; now, a large stooped figure in old-fashioned walking shoes, slanting a bit to the right at the podium, he still conveyed that same energy and passion. His blue eyes radiated hope and enthusiasm.

David spoke about turning the lights on for our future. He told his famous World War II story, about a time when turning lights on had saved his life. The war had just ended, and when the sun went down, the Germans began to shell David's battalion (the infamous 10th Mountain Division). Clearly, the Germans hadn't heard the news. So in order to avoid further casualties, David's unit turned on the headlights of their vehicles. No one had ever consciously done this while in battle. No doubt realizing that something odd was going on, the Germans ceased their fire.

When David finished speaking, I stood and clapped with the rest until my hands hurt. Then they were calling my name.

I blundered up to the podium on autopilot, taking in as much air as possible, then slowly letting it out. I'm sure the audience could hear the air hiss from my lungs over the large overhead black speakers. The video camera operator flipped a switch, and the light changed from red to green. I was on.

I put my hands in my pockets and looked out at all the upturned faces. My silence had captured their attention. I could hear plates being cleared in a room across the hall. The air conditioning system was humming. I looked up at the skylight twelve stories up and took a deep breath.

"It's not too late," I began, and immediately felt the words start to come, start to tumble from my mouth. I went on, hardly knowing what I said; all I did know was that my heart was full, and as I spoke, heads were nodding all over the room. I finished with a quote from my favorite Jewish scholar, Abraham Joshua Heschel:

As a tree torn from the soil, as a river separated from its source, the human soul wanes when detached from what is greater than itself.

Without the holy, the good turns chaotic, without the good, beauty becomes accidental.

It is attachment to what is spiritually superior, loyalty to a sacred idea, devotion to a noble friend or teacher, love for one's people or for humankind, which holds our inner life together.

Unless we aspire to the utmost, we shrink into inferiority.

The applause was loud, the audience on its feet. Ray Anderson came over and hugged me. Then a dozen others did. "I love the way you think," David Brower said as he wrapped his huge arms around me and squeezed. Wow. Incredible. Something huge had happened, but I wasn't sure what.

By mid-1999, membership in the council was growing (it hit 250 that May) as was interest in the LEED green building rating system. Since the San Diego conference three years earlier, Kristin had run the council's day-to-day activities, first out of my office on New Montgomery Street, and then out of new offices at 110 Sutter Street, where I had a seventh-floor suite and she had set up the council's office on the fourth floor. Two other staff members helped out, but we were always shorthanded.

"You need to be more constructive with me," Kristin blurted out one evening at the office. I'd been admonishing her to bring in more members and make more public appearances. She tended to stay in the office with her head in the paperwork. "I'm doing my best. If you think we need someone else for the job, then bring in somebody," Kristin went on. She was red and shaking. She looked tired, as if she hadn't slept for a week.

I stared at my shoes, keeping silent.

On my drive home, I realized that I'd pushed Kristin as far as I could. She'd done a tremendous job, but the council needed something more. I was spending time I didn't have supervising her. We'd also grown beyond my capabilities and limited non-profit experience.

The next day I wrote a memo to the board, saying it was time we brought in a president (we hadn't had one since I'd resigned from that role in 1994). I showed it to Kristin, hoping desperately that she wouldn't quit. Without her, we wouldn't have an organization worthy of bringing in a president.

When she finished reading it, she looked up. "I've always wanted what's best for the council. Send it out."

Several months later, in late 1999, the board assembled in San Francisco for a quarterly meeting. We'd rented the Carnelian Room, on the top—52nd—floor of the Bank of America Building near the council's offices. Everyone was in a good mood; we were excited to see each other, the panoramic views of the city below were spectacular, the coffee and the food were good. But the cause of our good spirits went beyond that.

Steven Winter, our newly elected chairman who'd just replaced Rick Fedrizzi after his six-year reign, nodded at a smiling woman sitting to his right at the board table. "Our new president and CEO, Christine Ervin," he announced. Everyone clapped and beamed. Kristin was clapping too. Christine, who was in her mid-forties, had been President Clinton's Assistant Secretary of Energy, overseeing nearly a thousand employees. Before that, she'd been the director of energy for Oregon.

She'd spoken in 1996 at our third annual green building conference in San Diego, an event we cohosted with AIA and NIST. "I envision every building as its own renewable power plant," she'd said then; and now, stepping gracefully into her new role, she said, "The council has always been dear to my heart. I'm flattered and excited to lead this incredible organization and group of pioneers into the next century."

CHAPTER 12

A Zealot? Me?

IN JUNE 1998 a new office tower was being designed for California's EPA headquarters in downtown Sacramento. The twenty-five-story building totaled over one million square feet and would take up an entire city block. As reported in the *Los Angeles Times,* many people wondered whether the building would be green.

One day, I received a call from the office of state assembly-woman Deborah Bowen. The state wanted to hire me. It took me several seconds to find my voice. I couldn't have been more flab-bergasted if I'd seen a hundred-foot-long purple dinosaur float past my tenth-floor window. The biggest new public building in California, and I was being asked to steer it green!

Unfortunately, I got so caught up in my messianic passion that I came very close to screwing up the project and jeopardizing my consulting future with the state.

The state's Department of General Services issued a press release announcing my contract: "Gottfried is a leader in environmental design. We are pleased to bring such forward-thinking people with expertise on environmentally smart buildings into this process," Cal/EPA secretary Peter Rooney was quoted as saying.

I hired the largest green team I'd ever assembled—two energy experts, two green architects, and my own cost estimator. I wasn't going to hold back on this one, even if it meant I didn't make any money. I asked my team to develop three levels of green: ideal, middle of the road, and low. Of course, I wanted ideal.

Thomas Development Partners (TDP), a major firm based in L.A., was the developer. Jim Thomas was a friend of Governor Pete Wilson's and owner of the Sacramento Kings hockey team. His company had already been working on the project for years before I came along. The building's exterior and base building design, after many hearings, had been publicly approved. That made it nearly impossible to change.

TDP had an agreement with the state providing for shared savings from any cost reductions below the guaranteed maximum price of $170 million. The last thing in the world Thomas wanted was me in there driving the costs up. But that was something that, initially, I deliberately cast aside. I was all about green, and the more the better. I envisioned another L.A. Times article, several years out: "The State's Greenest Building." The photo would show a fuel cell on the grass roof, with translucent photovoltaic solar cells integrated into the façade. Naturally, there would be a picture of me as well.

"This is the one," I told my green team on a conference call. "I want all of your most creative ideas." Our initial building energy analysis showed that the building as designed was at 24 percent below the energy code. I was surprised it was that efficient—the state and TDP team must have made energy a priority. However, it only scored fourteen LEED points: twelve short of the lowest certification level. We could boost that score, we discovered, by redesigning some systems and going stringently green with the tenant improvements, which hadn't yet been designed.

I soon had several different schemes for the building. One of them hit LEED Gold, increasing energy efficiency to 41 percent below code with the help of an underfloor air distribution system, solar cells, a fuel cell, and individually tuned windows on every side of the building. We'd even brainstormed a mechanical solar tracking panel on the roof that would follow the sun's movement during the day.

Then John Goleman phoned. He was the state's Department of General Services manager for the project and my client. To my surprise, he wanted to come over the next day to talk to me. I'd been sketchy about keeping him up to date on our work, and I hadn't gotten around to mentioning my goal of hitting LEED Gold. (I'd read the state's design-build agreement with TDP, and the contractual references requiring Thomas's creation of a green building were weak, requiring only a "best efforts" approach. In my experience, that type of language never added up to much.)

John showed up at my office at around three the next afternoon. He sat stiffly at the Italian glass conference table, his arms crossed. "What are your plans for the brainstorm?" he asked.

I told John that we'd come up with three tiers of alternatives and were going to recommend LEED Gold. He gasped. "David," he said, "most of the building is already designed. We've been working on it for five years." I sat back in my chair and bit the end of my pen so hard I thought the ink would squirt into my mouth. "The only thing open for consideration is the tenant improvements. They haven't been designed yet."

"The building should have an underfloor air distribution system, more efficient glazing, and a higher level of insulation," I countered. "It's a good investment over the life of the building. The underfloor air system boosted energy efficiency by 8 percent in our Santa Monica project. It also improves indoor air quality and user flexibility."

He visibly struggled to stay calm. "That's out of the question."

I turned red with rage. "Assemblywoman Bowen brought me in to do a good job. I'd hoped that you would give me the latitude to do that." I was struggling with my own anger now, let down that I'd be unable to deliver a showcase green building.

"You work for me," John said.

There was silence. Out of the corner of my eye I saw a red and white tanker glide up the bay. "Do you know Joe Rodota?" I asked. Joe was deputy chief of staff for the governor. We'd met twenty years ago at Stanford, and I'd last run into him in 1990 skiing in Vail. "Joe's an old fraternity brother of mine. I assume you know that Anne Sheehan is his wife?" (Anne was acting secretary of the State and Consumer Services Agency. Her immediate boss was the governor. John's entire agency, the Department of General Services, fell under her command.)

John looked at me like I'd hit him. "We can work this out ourselves," he said. When I said nothing, he rose. "Well, I hope you understand where I'm coming from."

Two days later my project manager, Huston Eubank, and I raced up to Sacramento in my Z3 for a BuildingCamp brainstorm session for the Cal/EPA building, chitchatting the entire way, excited and nervous. I'd even put on a tie. We expected about one hundred people: the full building design team, including the architects, A. C. Martin, and engineers, Levine Seegal; the developer; and representatives from the various EPA agencies that would be tenants in the building, such as the Integrated Waste Management Board. We parked outside the SMUD (Sacramento Municipal Utility District) building. I'd chosen to meet there because it had an underfloor air system and other innovative technologies—hoping it would inspire the attendees. SMUD had also participated with my green team to generate renewable energy ideas and incentives for the building.

The room began to fill up. I said hello to a few people I knew and was making my way to the front when my way was blocked by Mike Smith, senior vice president for TDP. We'd never met before, but I knew who he was. He was thick and burly, with a big neck below a bright-red face.

"This is my project," he spit out, his face close to mine, "and I'm setting the ground rules." I took a step backward. "The base building is not up for discussion. If you want to accomplish anything, you'll stick to the tenant improvements."

I felt the wind go out of me. As my lungs emptied, my anger shot up. "It may be your project, but it's my meeting. I was brought in to brainstorm, and you've no right to limit the discussion." He stomped to his seat. I realized I was shaking.

A few moments later, we called the meeting into session. I started off by having several manufacturers talk about renewable energy systems that would work for the building, a topic of interest to all. "We can design the building so that a fuel cell can plug into the building at a later date when it's feasible," said the lead architect from A. C. Martin. The mood in the room was cautious and edgy, and discussion remained limited—making the session more presentational than participatory. My team of experts offered suggestions, the developer's design team took notes. There couldn't have been more of a difference from the vibrant, almost jubilant integrated dialogue we'd had a few months earlier on the Santa Monica Public Safety Facility project.

At sunrise the next morning, I put on running shoes and headed out on a trail along the American River near our hotel. I ran for an hour, and to my surprise, my stride and breathing were in harmony. My thinking was clear. As I showered after the run, I felt a rare sense of peace. I dressed and returned to the meeting room for round two. "Today, each of us faces an opportunity and a choice," I said quietly, grabbing hold of the lectern and staring deep into the eyes of my listeners. "When you go home tonight, I want you to ask yourself if you pushed yourself toward greatness, or mediocrity."

That day we brainstormed dozens of wish-list ideas, including lighting at 0.8 watts per square foot, product emissions testing and imposed off-gassing emission limits, end-use electrical metering, permanent air monitoring, building commissioning, and a dual-plumbing gray-water system for the bathrooms. Meanwhile, both my client and the developer sat silently with their arms crossed. The next time I looked over, John Goleman's seat was empty. I never saw him again.

"You're a zealot," remarked one of the EPA participants in the parking lot afterward. "Even if you try, you can't control yourself."

Me? A zealot? The label irked me, but over time I came to recognize the truth of it. Once when I played football in high school, the noseguard for a competing team decked me. After the play, I got up and, slowly and shakily, made my way back to the team huddle. I sucked in air and chanted *Kill!* in my mind. On the next play I drove straight at the three-hundred-pounder, hitting him an inch above the ankles. He fell over, bounced once, and settled to the ground. Even as pain shot through me, I smiled. I'd done it. I put both hands on the ground to push myself up, then screamed in agony. I'd dislocated both shoulders. It was the end of my football career.

Had I done a similar thing here? Even as I wondered, I didn't care. I reminded myself I was on the side of the angels.

A week later I received a nasty letter from Mike Smith telling me that in his "wildest dreams" he couldn't fathom why we continued to demand changing the building to accommodate an underfloor air delivery system and other base building design changes, like the windows.

I shot an answer back to John Goleman; "My wildest dreams," I wrote, "are unfortunately big. I dream for a state of California that demonstrates environmental leadership through its actions and boldness, not words. I dream of team collaboration and integration to create healthy, productive buildings that consume minimal energy, contribute to a world of less pollution and waste." I then added, "I believe we can do all of this and still have it work on a life-cycle costing basis at a rate of return higher than the state's cost of capital." I copied the letter to the state secretaries of EPA and State and Consumer Services, Assemblywoman Bowen, and Jim Thomas. In my anger, I chose to not send a copy to Mike Smith.

Mike Italiano had given me *The Art of War* when we were building the council. In my fury, I'd forgotten one of the famous ancient warrior Sun Tzu's key lessons: "Supreme excellence consists in breaking the enemy's resistance without fighting." I was not mature enough to understand. I was still making diving tackles that brought not only my opponent down, but myself as well.

Anne Sheehan called when she got my letter. "Let's meet and resolve this thing, David," she said. "In the meantime, I assume you'll hold off from sending any further letters."

"Yes, of course," I said, feeling elated. "Green" would now receive a hearing at the highest level.

The day before the meeting, I went for a sunrise bike ride in the Marin Headlands. I crossed the Golden Gate Bridge and climbed the steep hill, shifting into my granny gear. Sweat dripped down my face and back. At the summit, I stopped and looked at the city skyline, all Mediterranean whites and pastels except for the black rectangle of the Bank of America building. It was so quiet and peaceful there. A breeze cooled my brow and rattled the manzanita. Why did I need this fight? I didn't own the building. I breathed in the salty air. Once it had filled my lungs, I exhaled — letting it all go.

Later that morning in the office, I directed Huston Eubank to select only the most practical ideas, those that respected the stated project constraints. I then trekked out to Sacramento to apologize to Mike Smith for the letter I'd written. He said, "We'll do our best to add as much of the green as possible. You have my word."

I had nothing further to do with the building. A few years later, in late 2001, I stood in front of the tower. Its massive size overwhelmed my senses. I pulled out my camera and took several digital photos. The developers had installed the solar cells on the roof of the building and incorporated many green finishes into the tenant improvements: low-emitting paint, carpet tile with a high level of recycled content, and superefficient lights. The building ended up 29 percent more energy efficient than the code requirement.

Other projects followed. One of the tenants of the Cal/EPA building was the California Integrated Waste Management Board. Ralph Chandler, the board's executive director, and Arnie Sowell, the assistant to the board member Dan Eaton, had been at the two-day Cal/EPA building brainstorm session, and had hired me as the CIWMB's green building advisor. Over the next three years, on their behalf, I went on to advise the greening of seventeen projects for local governments in the state.

I was also involved in the state's next major project, the Capitol Area East End: a $400 million, five-building, 1.5-million-square-foot complex. Here, we learned from the Cal/EPA and other projects by including a strong green requirement from inception in the bidding requirements and evaluation criteria for hiring the design-build contractor. As a result, the finished project beat the energy code by 30 percent by installing "cool" roofs, environmental systems furniture, an underfloor air distribution system, and dozens of other green building enhancements. One of the five buildings earned California's second LEED Gold certification.

In 2000 I was hired by another waste board, Alameda County Waste Management Authority, representing fourteen cities in the East Bay. Ann Ludwig, their senior program manager, challenged me to design a course on the greening of city contracts for retaining architects, engineers, contractors, and developers. When I told her I'd never done such a thing, she said, "I know. That's why I hired you."

I spent the entire next month, including several all-nighters, working to write a three-hundred-page manual, illustrated by 120 slides. It showed how to green a six-hundred-page design-build contract that Alameda County General Services Administration had given me to use as a prototype. Contract greening was a rewarding new task that allowed me to draw on my experience in many areas: development, construction, legal contracts, building design, and green buildings.

When the government starts throwing money at anything green, it's human nature to get in line. I am not immune to this. In a sense, that's how I got into green building myself, when Congress was funding those early green demonstration projects and Mike and I formed the council to, in part, get in on the action. Yes, I was already passionate about green buildings, but bucks are green too, and I'd be lying if I said I never noticed that.

But I was not the only one—or the worst. In mid-2002 I was invited to Bozeman, Montana, for a two-day green brainstorm meeting at the hunting lodge of a developer named Bill Lamb. A dozen other "greenies" had also been invited—experts in the areas of energy, water, development, and design. We were met at the Bozeman airport by one of Bill's project staff. On leaving the main highway about an hour's drive outside of town, we drove for about ten minutes on a dirt road, through thousands of acres of vegetation and man-made lakes, toward the hunting lodge. We passed deer, wild turkeys, and, in the marsh areas, statuesque white cranes. We drove by several farms and ranch houses. As Bill assembled his kingdom, he'd purchased some twenty-five individual parcels, allowing many of the sellers to retain their homes free of charge, if they agreed to work for him on the compound and miles of newly created preserves, including a hunting and fishing resort.

Emerging from the woods, I gained our first view of the place. It was massive, an oversized mix of hunting lodge and fortress constructed of enormous logs and boulders. The dark structure stood adjacent to a huge man-made lake, which visitors were compelled to drive completely around to access the compound. The lodge's entrance was twelve or more feet in height, looking like the front of a castle with its four-inch-thick wooden door. To the left was a retinal scanner. "Sometimes he can't find his key," the driver remarked.

On entering the building, I found myself in what felt like a medieval great room, about two thousand square feet in extent, with ceilings thirty feet high. The floors were all stone. Dozens of huge log beams were exposed throughout, some up to eight feet in circumference. Full-size canoes and other antiques hung from the beams.

We toured about a half dozen rooms on the second floor, each with a different theme. They, too, were massive, with high ceilings and large private bathrooms. They looked like miniature houses in their own right. The decorating budget could easily have been $150,000 or more per room.

Our group of experts had been assembled to provide strategic guidance in the greening of a project Bill envisioned creating outside Dallas: the world's largest shopping mall, along with a dozen hotels and office buildings. The mall alone would be ten million square feet—an artificial city under a single roof. And he wanted it to be better than LEED Platinum. "I want Dallas Center to use zero fossil fuel and be a net energy generator," he declared when we had all convened in a well-appointed conference room, next to the thirty-seat state-of-the-art theater. "It will be the greatest showcase for renewable technology in the world. The cost is over $2 billion." The sketchy renderings of the envisioned project made it look like a mix of Disneyland and Biosphere II.

"I have the money. I have been fortunate. My children are successful in their own right and they don't need my money. I am prepared to put in whatever it takes, even if the green adds hundreds of millions. What I am missing is the knowledge; that's why I invited you here. What *you* have been missing is a committed owner with the capital and connections to make things happen."

He took a sip of water and surveyed the room. "I am seeing the governor on Sunday. I need your help in figuring out what points to emphasize. He loves this project and is very supportive. When finished in twenty years, this project will bring one hundred thousand jobs and fifty million people each year to Texas." That didn't sound very environmental to me.

Next he turned to the need to eradicate our dependence on foreign oil, becoming passionate, raising his voice and waving his arms. He almost couldn't contain himself. All of the green experts in attendance were firm advocates of reducing America's energy consumption and boosting renewable energy generation. However, we weren't billionaires. Most of us couldn't reach top politicians. We didn't own thirty million square feet, as this man did, and so we couldn't create our own market as we "greened" fifteen million square feet of commercial space.

We were each invited to make recommendations for the mall, its other buildings, and how to make its energy systems self-sufficient and renewable. But we never got a chance: The agenda seemed to change every minute, despite the careful advance preparation of the staff. Bill kept switching direction, listening for a while, and then, when he couldn't sit silently any longer, launching into another speech—making it clear that we weren't getting at what he envisioned. Some of the participants had questioned the volume of traffic the project would attract and our ability to achieve LEED Platinum, given its unprecedented size. "I want you to be positive and creative," he admonished at the end of the first day. "I don't want to hear why we can't do this, but what we *can* do."

Despite Bill's urging that we redouble our efforts the next day, again the opportunity to do constructive work never arose. First thing in the morning he sat down with our panel and asked us to come up with the presentation for the governor's meeting on Sunday. But when we tried to do this, he changed tack and decided we needed a mission statement for the various project components.

At day's end, I still had not presented my ideas for the project, so one of Bill's staff called him over to see the slides I'd been asked to prepare in advance. It was my main opportunity to reach him, and to contribute to the project. "You have two minutes," Bill told me. "They're waiting for us to come to dinner."

I tried to focus and speak as quickly as possible. Already with the first slide, though, I saw that he wasn't with me, but was looking off to the hallway where others were talking. I quickly and mechanically read him the titles of my slides and finished before the two-minute deadline.

Bill's project manager approached me a short while later at the dinner table. "David, can you come with me?"

"What's up?"

"We want you to come to a press briefing upstairs. The local media want to learn about the project. Can you tell them your thoughts about the development, from the perspective of the founder of the U.S. and World Green Building Councils?" Immediately I felt flushed, as my stomach dropped to the floor. They hadn't told us that we'd be asked to provide a testimonial to the media. I wondered if Bill had assembled us "greenies" much as he had the stuffed animals and antiques adorning his castle. I imagined that with his wealth he could do whatever he desired.

"Sure, no problem." I understood I was expected to be supportive and say that both projects were credible world-class examples of sustainable building—even though we had not seen any plans and the first team of architects had been fired. Other than hearing the enormous goals and vision of the owner, I really knew nothing about the project. We were necessary in order to affirm his credibility with government and the press, and even more important, to get enormous governmental subsidies.

It all came down to making his project the biggest, grandest, greenest vision imaginable, attracting the right people—politicians and idealists with deep pockets—and then opening the sluice gates so the money would pour in. And it would: This man was a true marketer, with the know-how and the connections to make his vision reality.

I kept my cool and made the most of the social interaction with my colleagues until it was time to leave the next morning. I had a hard time falling asleep that last night, as I tried to make sense of the extravaganza while staring at a stuffed turkey, beaver, and wild boar above the ballast fireplace in my room. I'd learned at Cal/EPA that it's important to accept gray, rather than always push for white (with the strong likelihood that all you'll get is black). Dallas Center, however, was too close to black from the outset, and I decided to watch from afar.

CHAPTER 13

Show Me the (Internet) Money!

"WELCOME TO Garage.com Boot Camp," read the banner overhead at the San Francisco Conference Center near the airport. It was September 1999, the height of the Internet craze. I fought my way through the thousand other entrepreneurs, vying for a seat at the front. This was hardly the "exclusive" session that had been advertised. I should have brought my binoculars.

All around the Bay Area, start-ups were getting millions for the sketchiest of ideas. Lawyers, bankers, graduate students, and professors were abandoning their occupations to join these fledgling companies—everybody knew how much receptionists who worked for Netscape had made in stock options before they retired. "Did you hear about Val Vaden?" one of my Stanford friends asked me at a reunion. "He's made a fortune." Val, one of our SAE fraternity brothers, was a founding general partner at Benchmark Capital, the venture capital firm that took eBay and Ariba public. The next week I saw his picture in the *San Francisco Chronicle*. He and his wife were selling a house they'd never occupied: The price tag was $9 million.

So here I was, getting in line with the rest. My idea was a business-to-business hub for buying the best green building products at the lowest price. I had little trouble arranging meetings with venture firms. A few of my Stanford classmates were venture capitalists—VC's—in Menlo Park, along Sand Hill Road, the epicenter for such firms. At times, thanks to all that money, Sand Hill Road looked like an exotic car dealership, what with all the Porsches, Ferraris, and BMWs parked on its flanks.

I not only made the speech of the new economy part of my vocabulary—talking with ease about options, IPO's, term sheets, and Internet exchanges—but I had all the right accessories as well: khakis and a golf shirt, hair gel, Rolex watch, BMW convertible, Blackberry wireless PDA. Every surface in my apartment held piles of the Internet bibles: *Red Herring*, *Wired*, *Fast Company*, and the *Industry Standard*. I couldn't read each issue fast enough. My fantasies grew with each rise of the stock market. First I thought I needed $1 million to make a go of it. Then $10 million.

As each VC appraised my business plan, I'd gleefully calculate my potential net worth, just as I'd done in the '80s making real estate deals. I learned about stock options and strike prices when a firm went public. I dreamed of the things the new paper wealth would buy: a custom-designed house in San Francisco and a retreat in Inverness, near Point Reyes—both rated LEED Platinum, of course. Greed had lain dormant in my soul, and now it was back, but this time I'd merged it with "green."

That's not what I told myself at the time, of course. I wasn't after greenbacks; I was "greening" the Internet highway.

In early 2000 I gave a speech at PG&E's Pacific Energy Center on Howard Street called "Greening Greed." I opened with a video clip from the 1987 movie *Wall Street*, when Gordon Gekko, played by Michael Douglas, gives his "Greed is good" speech. "Greed is right," he says. "Greed works. Greed clarifies, cuts through, and captures the essence of the evolutionary spirit.

Greed, in all of its forms—greed for life, for money, for love, knowledge—has marked the upward surge of mankind." Then I showed the scene from *Jerry Maguire* when the young sports broker screams, "Show me the money!"

"Whether we like it or not, it's all about money," I told the audience. Some in the crowd of a hundred or so were my friends; most were greenies who always came to the energy center lectures. "We should harness the power of the Internet to help us green the world." My listeners looked perplexed, as if they'd gone out for popcorn and come back to find the wrong movie playing. The reaction to my talk was flat. No one said, "Very inspirational," as I sometimes heard at my lectures. Several people did give me their business cards and ask for jobs once WorldBuild.com was funded. Others asked if I was accepting angel investors. At one point, I thought I'd gather all of the greenies into a single investment pool, creating our own public offering. Real Goods Trading Company had done that, and raised about $7 million.

I met with a lot of VC's. Donna Novitsky, an acquaintance from Stanford and now a partner at Mohr Davidow Ventures, agreed to hear my spiel. One of her other partners, George Zachary, had been on the cover of *Red Herring* the week before. A guy waiting with me in the reception area was wearing a solid gold Rolex. He'd slid his shiny new $100,000 black Porsche 911 Carrera Cabriolet in next to my dirty $40,000 BMW Z3 in the parking lot.

"We want to move fast on this one," Donna said after I'd presented my proposal. "I'd like you to meet Rob Chaplinsky, one of our general partners."

I drooped. "Oh, I see," I said. I'd been through this drill several times, including once with Val's firm. I did well with my first pitch, and then got dinged in round two. A few times, I'd even made it to round three, but never further. After the first meeting, they'd ask me hard questions. Who's on your team? What's your experience in technology? Have you written a business plan yet? Have you run financials? Why is this an Internet play?

After each meeting, I'd sprint, trying to come up with answers. I called friends to see if they would leave their jobs and join me if I got funded. "You'll get lots of stock options," I promised them. When they asked about salary and benefits, I'd say, "Don't worry about that, the stock options are what's important. Later on we'll have lots of money for other things." That was the answer I'd learned from others who had made it in the new field.

As I could have predicted, the meeting with Donna's partner didn't go well. "How do you differ from the other three firms in the building industry that have already been funded?" he wanted to know. He'd kept up to date on Autodesk's buzzsaw.com and Bidcom.com—each of which had raised almost $100 million. Another building industry digital firm, Cephren, was also in the running at the time. I'd met with all three companies, and narrowed in on buzzsaw.com. I liked their linkage to Autodesk (the global leader in CAD software), and a Stanford friend, Anne Bonaparte, was one of the founders. She loved the green approach, but we hadn't yet worked out how our partnership might work. At each meeting, I asked for more than they were prepared to invest. Despite their seemingly bursting coffers, they were always in survival mode and not ready to put cash or up-front equity on the table for me.

"The other building industry Internet firms are laying the digital highway for the industry. I'm going to use the highway to ship high-performance green building products to my community," I said as the VC began fidgeting with his pen as if it was the newest invention.

He stopped. "What's green building?"

As I described it, he put his pen down on his notepad and glanced at the clock on the wall. Its second hand was ticking so loud I lost my train of thought.

"Have you thought of going to one of the social venture funds?"

I began to pack up my presentation materials. "Yes, I met with Baccharis Capital last week," I said. I'd met with Noel Perry, the managing director. He explained that they were out of money: Their entire $25 million fund had already been invested. I had also called Calvert Social Fund—they too were out of investment funds. The week before, another Stanford SAE friend at Oak Investment had also rejected me. Their latest technology fund was capitalized with $3 billion.

"Well," Rob now said as he showed me to the firm's reception area, "I think we'll sit this one out."

I started to feel that I didn't have enough words in my vocabulary to convince a VC to fund me. They wanted to invest in conventional-sector deals like Internet infrastructure and networking and communications. Some had even invested in retail service companies such as Webvan, whose initial public offering raised $375 million to deliver groceries ordered over the Internet. They then committed over $1 billion to construct twenty-six food warehouses, before going bankrupt.

One day as I sat editing my VC PowerPoint presentation down from thirty slides to eight (I had finally learned that I needed to get my idea across faster), my assistant, Michelle Crozier, said over the intercom that an analyst from Bank of America was on the phone.

It was Chris Hartung, managing director of real estate research with Banc of America Securities, a subsidiary of Bank of America Corporation, the largest real estate lender in the world.

"We own 3,500 buildings for our bank branches," Hartung said. "Environmental performance has always been one of our concerns. Can we meet?"

Jackpot!

A few days later, Chris showed up at my office with a colleague. It was January 2000. Investors were now interested in B2B's — Business to Business exchanges — and that was what I was creating for the world's largest industry. I walked them through my new PowerPoint presentation. We talked for two hours about the prospects for an Internet play in green building. "We'd like to enter into a formal due diligence review of your new business," Chris said at the end of the meeting. "We'll need a full business plan."

"When do you want it?" I asked.

"Thirty days."

That night I treated myself to a steak dinner at Izzy's in the Marina.

For the next thirty days I stayed home, beavering away at the business plan as my toast burned, coffee grew cold, a beard sprouted, and laundry piled up. I sent the thirty-page plan to Chris, who called me at home to say he liked it. I had dashed out of the shower to answer my phone, and stood dripping on the kitchen floor. "That's fantastic," I said, a grin splitting my face. "What's the next step?"

"We'll want to do more research on the field and have some more meetings with you. You'll need to build a team and find a head of technology. We think you can run the business as the founder/CEO, but you'll need help before we can fund you."

"When do you think I'll get a term sheet?" I asked. I'd learned that until you got a letter detailing the amount of funding, company valuation, and other business terms, the investor wasn't serious.

"We'll need a coinvestor before we commit to any funds," Chris said. "One of the VC firms you've been talking to would be great."

Ouch!

Chris introduced me to a new venture firm that served as an incubator for entrepreneurs like me—the ones who needed hand-holding. The firm was called Twelve and funded by Eric Greenberg. But it turned out they were interested only in technology plays.

Then a VC at Accel Partners referred me to a private investor who'd made a fortune taking his firm public. His name was Robert Glass, and he'd gone to Stanford at the same time I did.

In March 2000 Robert and I met at Buck's restaurant in Woodside, the hub of venture capital activity. I arrived early and took a large booth, facing the doorway so I could try to pick Robert out. All around me VC's in golf shirts were talking about deals they'd funded—or listening to nervous entrepreneurs like me, interrupted every few minutes by a VC's ringing cell phone. We were the hungry, and they controlled the food supply.

As I waited, I spun dreams in my head. Once I'd amassed great wealth, I would use the money to change the system. I'd create an incubator that nurtured green firms. Instead of trying to fit into the limited valuations of the NASDAQ, I would help invent the next stock market, the Green Exchange. The highest-valued firms would be those that were helping to restore our water, air, and depleted resource base. It was pie-in-the-sky thinking, I know; green capitalism may be an oxymoron. But I was still an idealist at heart.

In walked Robert. His stringy blond hair was covered with a baseball cap that said "Gone Fishing." I waved, and he came over and sat down. "Do you like to fish?" I asked, intrigued. I was still recovering from poison oak from a trip the week before with a cousin, fly-fishing for wild trout in the McCloud River. "Yes, it's one of my passions," he said. "My ranch in Montana has ten miles of river frontage." The coffee I'd just sipped almost came back out my nose.

As I gave him my quick pitch, Robert pulled out a pen and began writing on his napkin. After about five minutes he held up a hand and said, "I get it. Let me tell you how I rate companies. I've invested in about fifteen over the past two years. If they meet my test, I start with a $500,000 investment."

I nodded, and he continued. "I use a simple point system. I rate the new company in five areas, assigning a value from 0 to 20 for each. If I get a number higher than 85, I invest."

He grabbed his napkin and wrote down his five assessment categories. "I'm going to rate your firm," he said. "The five categories are: market size, entrepreneur experience, team, ability to harness the power of the Internet, and market positioning." I sat up a little straighter. I liked his system and his no-nonsense approach. My heart pumped wildly.

"I give you a 20 for market size: the building industry is enormous." He wrote a 20 on the napkin. "You've started several organizations, which is good, but you haven't scaled a business and taken it public. I give you a 15 for experience." That number was jotted down. "It sounds as if you've lined up a good prospective team, but you're weak in the technology area. I give you a 15 for team." I began tapping my right foot as he added that figure to the list. "I like your idea of aggregating buyers of green products from your community, and your plan to start with the public sector. I can see it building over time. The new B2B exchange tools, and the ability to harness product data, make this a solid Internet play." He jotted down a 15. "From what you say, you will be the first to market commercial green building products on the Web. I give you a 20 for this category," he said, then added up the numbers. "Your total is 85. This meets my initial threshold." I sat up, almost coming out of my shoes. Was he going to write me a check?

"What does that mean? Where do we go from here?" I asked.

"We'll need other investors. I'd like to meet with the folks at Bank of America and also introduce you to a few venture firms that I coinvest with."

Over the next few months, from February through May 2000, I worked at furthering the deals with Robert and Bank of America. Each wanted me to get a commitment from the other before moving forward. Robert was busy with other deals and often off in Montana. It was hard to get his attention.

In April, a man named David Saltman, who worked for a small Canadian public company named Kafus Industries, came to a council meeting in D.C. to ask for support for an Internet business similar to the one I was proposing. His company made fiberboard and bio-composites from 100 percent discarded wood, and did not use the toxic urea formaldehyde as the glue to hold the wood fibers together. Purchasers of the products included Home Depot and large automotive companies. I admired how well David worked the room, but felt heated inside: This was my territory. How dare he invade?

The next week, David called me. He candidly explained his company's plans and the interest they'd had from Merrill Lynch, which had provided millions for Kafus. "We want to bring a green building product portal to the market. If we can better do this by joining forces, then let's do it. You can be the president," David said.

I'd be in charge. I liked that. The thought of Merrill Lynch and
Bank of America coming together on this was also compelling. I
had found the going lonely and costly. I'd already spent around
$100,000 building my Web site and for staff time to manage the
start-up efforts. Meanwhile, I'd been neglecting my consulting
business, which hurt our sales and billings.

I met with David and then his boss, Ken Swaisland, over coffee
at the Beverly Wilshire Hotel in L.A., and we agreed to split the
new company equity equally. They would even provide some
seed capital. As for our business plans, product specifications, and
other intellectual capital, those we would combine.

That week the stock market "crashed." It was May 2000. Internet
stocks began their rapid descent, falling as much as 90 percent.
Hundreds of billions of dollars' worth of paper value evaporated,
causing the portfolio values of venture capital firms to plummet.
Some lost billions in value.

I called Chris at Bank of America. "We're not sure what to
think," he said. "We're going to sit back and see what shakes out.
We've invested heavily in the Internet sector." He sounded
stunned. I told him about the possible merger with the Canadian
firm. "That sounds great," he said. "You need a stronger team and
CTO"—Chief Technology Officer. "It sounds as if they can provide those pieces. We've invested with Merrill Lynch on a few
deals. Let me know how it goes."

I flew up to Vancouver that week for a lunch meeting with Ken
Swaisland. I had a bad feeling in my stomach and had slept poorly
all week long.

Kafus Industries was located on the waterfront, with a view of
seaplanes landing and taking off. From the reception area I could

hear Ken on the phone. He'd taken five calls already while I waited. At one point he strode past me, grabbed his chief financial officer out of his office, and then the two hurried back down the hall. "Something's come up," he muttered to me as he rushed by. He was dressed like a Hollywood producer, in tweed sports jacket, custom white knit shirt, linen pants, and tasseled shoes.

When he finally came out to get me an hour later for our scheduled lunch, his forehead was sweaty and the wrinkles were showing. As we set off for a nearby restaurant, his cell phone rang. "No, let's just hold on for the rest of the day," he told the person on the other end. "We can't sell." He hung up and wiped his forehead with a monogrammed handkerchief. I was thinking I shouldn't have come.

"Someone's dumping shares of our stock," Ken said as I gulped down a diet Coke at the restaurant. His face was white. He threw back a martini and ordered another. His phone kept ringing. He ate his salmon in less than five minutes, put his fork down, and looked at me. "I need to get back to the office." I followed him at a slow trot back to Kafus. "We'll have to reschedule," he told me, then disappeared inside his office.

A few days later, I heard that Ken had been fired as chairman of his own company. When the stock price fell below $3 a share, their largest investor, Enron, decided to pull the plug. I later learned that they were not responsible for dumping stock, but they'd taken advantage of the situation. They wanted out of their extended liabilities as a partner in Kafus.

Within just a few days, not only had Ken's net worth dropped by $50 million, but he was out of a job. David was too. "Good luck," David said over the phone. "I'm sorry about the mess. I'm sure you'll land on your feet. As for me, I have no idea what I'm going to do." I admired his professionalism and honesty, even when our deal vanished.

Not long afterward, Chris Hartung left a message saying he was no longer working with Bank of America. He wished me well and gave a new contact name at the bank, but I never called it. I'd had enough!

CHAPTER 14
GBC Goes Global

"IT IS MY GREAT PLEASURE," I said, "to welcome the formation of the Japan Green Building Council!" I was standing on a stage in Tokyo; it was April 22, 1998—Earth Day. I wore a new lightweight sage-colored wool suit and a sparkling gold-patterned tie. My host, Takatoshi Ishiguro, had only seen me in my California wardrobe of jeans and Gap shirts and suggested that I should dress up. He was with PES International, a green building design and consulting firm.

I wore headphones so that I could hear the proceedings translated into English. It was my first time giving a speech through a translator. It seemed to take three seconds for them to turn my every one second of speech into Japanese, making me select every word carefully. Mr. Ishiguro had warned me to not tell jokes: "American humor doesn't work in Japan." I found his command difficult to obey; I like to stay loose on my feet.

Seated in front of me were about three hundred Japanese businessmen and government representatives, almost all of them wearing dark-blue suits with white shirts. It felt like the United States twenty years earlier. Several reporters took notes in the front row, and a video camera shined a bright light in my eyes, making me self-conscious.

I'd met Takatoshi Ishiguro three years earlier at the 1995 Big Sky, Montana, membership summit, the council's first exclusive gathering of its members. Previously, we'd hosted large conferences that were also open to the public. The summit concept excluded formal presentations; instead, we led discussions on critical green building topics. The session opened with an attempt to determine the council's first state-of-the-world summary of green building. Each of the three hundred attendees spoke for about thirty seconds on their efforts in green building. Hearing the collective stories of triumphs, challenges, obstacles, passion, and growth overwhelmed me. At that meeting, Ishiguro wore a suit and tie, while I had on shorts and a lightweight fishing shirt with "CalTrout" written on the pocket. He introduced himself in the formal Japanese way, extending his business card toward me with both hands and a slight bow of the head. I pulled out one of my cards and gave it to him the American way—in one hand without a bow.

"I want to found a green building council in Japan," he told me. "We are a different country and culture, but I think your model will work. Can you help me?" Earlier I'd noticed Mr. Ishiguro taking notes on a pad of pink Post-Its. (I later learned he'd been studying us for several years.) His thick black-rimmed glasses were dirty, and his hair slightly disheveled, as if he was too intent to take the time to attend to these basic niceties. On his jacket lapel was a round green pin with a Japanese character. I wondered what it signified.

As we spoke, I learned that he'd started an environmental discussion group in the city of Nagoya, where he lived, and wanted to expand beyond its hundred members, by adding from all parts of the industry, as a green building coalition like ours. They planned to create green building guidelines and host educational events. His assistant, Shisano Takeuchi, often spoke for him; although her English was easier to understand, his was quite good. He was an architect by training, and had worked for Syska & Hennesey, a medium-size U.S. engineering firm in New York (and an early member of the council).

Ishiguro and I stayed in touch for the next few years. We would meet in San Francisco during his frequent trips to the United States. He had scoured the country, tracking down many of our leading green building experts and projects. He had probably toured more American green buildings than I had. He'd also met many of the early pioneers, who were also my friends in the industry, and paid a few of them to lecture in Japan, as I was now doing.

He'd asked me to welcome the Japan council at this event, their inaugural meeting, and to give a talk on the economics of green building. "It's all about increased building value," I said as I almost wrapped up. "If a building is efficient in its use of resources, then its value will increase." I saw many heads nodding, but only about thirty seconds after I'd stopped speaking, while the translator caught up.

And here came my "kicker": "Now that we have green building councils in the U.S. and Japan, I'm announcing the formation of the World Green Building Council." I had come up with the idea on the flight over, figuring that if Japan was interested in the council model, other countries would be too. "The global building industry needs to work together to share knowledge, standards, and technologies. I hope you will join me." I looked out at the quiet room, feeling the way a ship's captain must have felt in the 1400s when landing on soil as yet untouched by Europeans. I

smiled broadly and held my head high. The next day my photo
appeared in the newspaper. I'm not sure what the caption said,
but it made me grin. Unfortunately, my only glimpse of Tokyo
was from the enormous Hilton Hotel, which was not much different than Hiltons in America, just bigger.

Ishiguro asked me to repeat my talk in Nagoya, and he also
arranged for a dozen or so meetings with government officials,
architects, and large product manufacturers. "What's the purpose
of this meeting?" I asked Shisano early on in our schedule, as we
headed into a small meeting room at the hotel after a quick breakfast of salad, fruit, and sushi. I was surprised to see about a dozen
business executives waiting for us. "They want to meet you,"
Shisano said. "Well, okay," I said, unsure of their intent.

We quickly got down to business, though for the most part I
had little role to play in the meeting. Occasionally they would
have a question for me: "David," Shisano translated, "they would
like to know about the cost of green building in the U.S. Is it
more?" For much of the discussion, however, I simply sat there,
trying to figure out what was going on. I heard my name mentioned occasionally, and the term "green building," but that was
about all I understood. Ishiguro was smiling and shaking his head,
talking fast as he led the discussion. I began to feel as if I was the
wriggling bait on the end of his fishing pole.

"I'm not sure what you're up to," I said to Ishiguro and Shisano
that night over dinner in the hotel restaurant. He'd had three
drinks already. Then he was yelling at her, or at least that's what it
sounded like. I sipped my Sapporo beer, not knowing what to
think. "We keep going to all these meetings. And it looks as if
you're drumming up work for your consulting business," I said.

He and Shisano jumped into a long exchange in Japanese. I sat and waited. Next time, I'd hire my own translator. The waiter had brought out a metal bowl and a small gas burner. Firing it up, he added water and about a dozen spices to the bowl. In no time it was boiling. He then placed a large platter of green vegetables and thinly sliced slabs of Kobe beef on the table. They called this dish *shabu-shabu*—which Shisano interpreted as meaning the "washing" of the vegetables and meat in the hot water. Eaten over rice with soy sauce, it looked more palatable than a few of the other meals I'd had in Japan, when I wasn't entirely sure if some of the things they served were even dead.

"We're very interested in working with you," Ishiguro said at last. "What is your standard billing rate?"

"Two thousand five hundred dollars per day," I said. "Plus expenses." I was actually billing at $2,000 per day at the time, but given the distance and cultural strain, I upped the amount.

"I see. That's expensive in Japan," Ishiguro said. Then he launched into another exchange with Shisano. Meanwhile, I "washed" more food in the hot water and stuffed the cooked items into my mouth. It was delicious.

"What services do you provide?" Ishiguro asked. Should I be frank? I was providing a free education, as I'd done over the past few years, coaching him on how to build a council. He'd paid me an honorarium and expenses for this visit and my talks, so at least I'd seen some cash, but for the most part all my advice had been free of charge. I hesitated, and then decided to trust him. Pulling out a pen, I made a list on the paper tablecloth of the various services I'd invented as part of my BuildingFutures program: the BuildingCamp brainstorming session, energy modeling using DOE software, life-cycle costing financial analysis, green materials research and selection, product procurement, peer review of building drawings at several levels of completion and building commissioning. "Can I keep this?" he asked once I'd finished, already beginning to fold up my work of "art." I nodded, and he put the paper in his shirt pocket along with the notes he'd scribbled while I was outlining my offerings.

For a year or two, I continued to meet with Ishiguro and Shisano when they came through San Francisco. During an international building rating system conference in Maastricht, Holland, I learned from two representatives from Takanaka, a large Japanese construction firm, that Ishiguro had trademarked the English term "green building" in Japan. That meant that whenever anyone wanted to use the term, they needed his approval. A few international green building leaders said I should not have permitted this. "If you want to be involved with the WorldGBC, you must release the trademark," I told Ishiguro and Shisano at lunch one day in San Francisco. A year later he had transferred the trademark to the Japan council, now a governmentally recognized nonprofit organization. (Why it hadn't started out as one I never did understand.)

After Japan came Korea. I'd heard about the formation of the Korea Green Building Council in 1998. From their material on the Web I could see that they'd copied the USGBC's organizational format and programs and Green Building Council name. The next year, three representatives from Korea came to my office. After an hour quizzing them about their ownership structure and bylaws, I'd learned that the Korea council was privately owned. "If you want to affiliate with us, you'll need to spin the council out into a nonprofit organization," I said. "Our model is open, consensus based, and strictly nonprofit." I was surprised when they agreed to do this, claiming that they hadn't fully understood our model.

A year later, I was pleased to hear from a governmental contact of mine in Seoul that he was now the chair of the newly established nonprofit council. Like us, they had started off by creating green building guidelines and a building rating system. I received photos of their first demonstration green building, housing the government's energy efficiency and research department. It looked as if it was from the 1980s, rather square, without much design detail, but it had extensive south-facing glazing with large solar shades and superefficient energy systems.

Next was Spain. In spring 1999, I'd had frantic e-mails and calls from a man named Aurelio Ramírez-Zarzosa, who wanted me to grant him the exclusive right to be the founder of the Spain Green Building Council. I was evasive: I'd never met the man, knew nothing about him. The WorldGBC was still just an idea in my head, even though I had announced it publicly. True, we had councils under way in the United States, Japan, and Korea, but no formal commitment to work together or a binding code of ethics. Nor, as I was acutely aware, did we have funds, staff, volunteer members, or a dues structure.

The two Spaniards came in July, and I met with them for two days. We had an enjoyable time and they seemed credible, so I agreed to work with them. Of course, they said that because they were just starting out, they had no funds to commit to the WorldGBC.

Just after the meetings with Aurelio, I got a call from the environmental director at Gap. She had $5,000 of extra funds in their foundation's year-end budget, and wanted to donate it to my council work. I told her about a founding WorldGBC meeting I was planning to hold that November, and she agreed to sponsor the event. It would be the first time representatives from the various countries with councils (plus a few others I had met over the years) came together.

About thirteen people representing six countries flew in for the two-day meeting. I had convinced Nigel Howard, director of the Center for Sustainable Construction at BRE in England (BRE developed the BREEAM rating system), to attend, and from Australia came Che Wall, a green building consultant I had met a few years earlier in Mexico when we lectured together for the Asia-Pacific Economic Cooperation Forum. Ishiguro and Shisano flew out from Japan, bringing their new council chairman. Aurelio returned with the partner I'd met previously from the Spanish green building council. We also had a representative from Russia whom I'd met the month before. Rick Fedrizzi, Mike Italiano, and Christine Ervin represented the USGBC. It felt great to have my comrades present as we incubated the next creation.

The evening after our first day of meetings, I hosted a celebratory dinner. "Thank you for bringing the vision of the green building council to your countries and for standing up as founders," I said to the group in our private banquet area at E & O Restaurant on Sutter Street, one of my favorites. The sound of the jazz pianist playing an old Benny Goodman tune wafted up from downstairs. Everyone was jovial, enjoying drinks after a productive day educating each other on their respective green building efforts. Those who already had councils shared their start-up experience with the newcomers. I felt at home with these kindred souls from many countries.

The second day was more difficult. I'd set a demanding agenda, hoping to address critical organizational issues: membership, founding board, rules of conduct, priority programs, and dues. "What's the purpose of the World Green Building Council?" Ishiguro asked at the beginning of the meeting. Since I'd known him for four years and he'd heard more than anyone present about the WorldGBC, I didn't understand why he was asking that, especially in such a challenging tone. I frowned at him, hoping he'd back down, but he met my look impassively. All eyes were on me.

"The WorldGBC is the umbrella organization for national green building councils," I replied. "Now, let's—"

Ishiguro had his hand up again. The room was tense. Our hostess came in with a pitcher to fill our water glasses. I waved her away. Finally I acknowledged Ishiguro with a curt nod of my head. "Whose hand is holding up the umbrella?" he asked.

I knew what he was implying, and I resented it. "No one country or person will own the WorldGBC. Each of us will have a seat on its board."

"But who will control the board?" he persisted. The others squirmed.

I had already explained to him several times that no one person or entity would control the nonprofit coalition's board. We would have officers, but the assembled group hadn't yet elected them, though I hoped that would happen by the end of the day. It was clear he thought that the USGBC and I would control the WorldGBC. To the contrary, I had taken great effort to prevent such a thing from happening. Instead of founding the world council from within the USGBC, I had set it up as a separate entity, inviting the U.S. council to assume only one seat on its board. The USGBC had agreed not only to this structure, but also to the principle that the world council would be rating system neutral: USGBC would not mandate that the WorldGBC use only LEED.

"You need to get control of yourself," my assistant, Michelle, whispered to me when I'd shown my rising frustration at the interruptions—and our overall lack of progress. My focus on organizational formation was distracting me from understanding the success of simply gathering as a world body of councils. I took a few deep breaths and plowed forward, managing to keep the rest of the meeting under control. In the end, we didn't come to any conclusions, but had a good discussion about the issues, and a few countries agreed to help fund a Web site for the WorldGBC.

There were other signs of growing interest in green building overseas. I went to China as part of a small U.S. group that had been invited by the Shanghai Overseas Returned Scholars Association to participate in the "Sustainable Shanghai" conference in July 2000. Accompanying me were Ray Anderson, of Interface, and Amory (and Hunter) Lovins from Rocky Mountain Institute. We each gave a short lecture to the four hundred or so assembled scholars and government officials. Amory and Hunter spoke about *Natural Capitalism*, the book they had just released with Paul Hawken. It had already been translated into Chinese, and I saw many of the scholars carrying it. (The word *capitalism* in the book's title had to be finessed, as it didn't translate well into the culture of our hosting country.) At a small session with several government officials, I talked about our experience in the United States with the USGBC and challenged them to create a similar entity in China. A few years later, I was pleased to learn that they had formed the Shanghai Green Building Alliance, in partnership with the Green Building Alliance of Pittsburgh, one of our early council members.

From Shanghai I flew to Hong Kong. I had set up several meetings with professors at Hong Kong University and was scheduled to deliver a few lectures on green building, including one for a small group from the Hong Kong Institute of Architects who were interested in forming a Hong Kong council. (Years later, in June 2003, the Professional Green Building Council of Hong Kong held its inaugural meeting.) I then had a beautiful lunch with Gordon Ongley, managing director of Swire Properties, a global developer of high-rise buildings. Swire's interest in green buildings surprised me. They owned an enormous chunk of land near the international airport, and were working with the city, which required use of their BEAM green building rating system (Hong Kong's version of England's BREEAM system), to make it into a model green community. During my meetings at Hong Kong University, the head of the journalism department asked me to accept an academic fellowship: I'd be able to teach, green their building, and write the book I had begun thinking about. The thought was appealing, but I still had things to do at home and wasn't ready to move halfway across the world.

Just before Christmas 2000 I flew to Madrid to meet with Aurelio and the three other founding partners of the Spain Green Building Council. They had sent me the airplane ticket, saying they had a business proposition to discuss that would help fund the WorldGBC.

In our first meeting, we exchanged progress reports on our respective councils. Membership in the USGBC was growing rapidly, having surpassed five hundred member firms and moving toward a thousand. The Spanish council had yet to officially form and had no funding, though they'd been at it for a year and a half. In that same time, the USGBC had raised several hundred thousand dollars.

Something was amiss.

One of the partners, Sergio Cruz, worked in a midsize legal firm in Madrid. Tall and about fifty pounds overweight, he'd walked in that morning wearing a shiny light-brown leather coat and looking more like a used car salesman than an attorney. We met in his firm's conference room, which stank of the cigarettes he was constantly smoking. When he wasn't lighting up, he was talking on his cell phone or with his secretary, who repeatedly interrupted us. I'd thought New Yorkers were wired, but this man and other Spaniards I met made them look like vacationers chilling on a beach. "Do you mind not smoking?" I'd asked him at the beginning of the meeting. "Sorry," he said equably, continuing to puff away. What kind of an environmentalist was this? And the others weren't much better. Ricardo García owned a family fish business in Biko, a small fishing town northwest of Madrid, and the third, Alfredo Rios, owned a landscape business. At least that was sort of connected to buildings. Aurelio was an engineer, and had been running the day-to-day business of the incipient council while carrying on his one-person consulting firm. His small, cluttered office in a shared suite reminded me of my own early days as a consultant.

I excused myself to go to the bathroom. A few seconds after I entered, the door opened and Aurelio came in. I turned to him. "What's going on?" I asked. "I've had enough of this bullshit." He didn't answer. The air smelled of urine, and paper towels littered the floor. Then he said in his thick Spanish accent, "They're playing with you, trying to figure out your position. They think you're weak, and they want to take advantage of you." He had bags under his eyes, and his tweed suit was wrinkled. "They've tied my hands for the past year. That's why we've accomplished nothing since we were in San Francisco."

"Why didn't you level with me before I flew all the way to Spain?" I asked, touching his shoulder to take the sting out of my words. I wanted to be angry with him, but he seemed defeated and in need of help.

"They said they wouldn't give me any money unless I got you here." He gazed at the floor for a few seconds, shaking his head. Then he looked at me. "I'm sorry that I wasn't honest with you. If you help me get rid of these three bozos, I'll make it up to you."

I studied the peeling paint on the toilet partition nearest me. "Okay," I said after a minute. "Let's do it."

As we entered the conference room, the three partners stopped talking. Maybe they sensed that something had changed.

"It's time you get to the point," I said in my Dirty Harry voice. "Why did you ask me here?" They looked at one other uneasily. "We propose to form a new business with you here in Spain and, if it works, expand it to cover the full European Union," the fish salesman said. Aurelio sat with his head down and his hands covering his face. He wanted me to handle this alone.

"I'm listening," I said to draw them out.

"We'll give you 20 percent of the new business, and we'll put in all the money."

"Un huh," I said after a few moments of silence. "What do you expect me to do for the 20 percent?"

"You deliver the LEED building rating system to us for Spain," he said. I sat back in my chair. This was the missing piece to the puzzle. Ironically, the USGBC had authorized me to negotiate a LEED licensing agreement with them.

"What are you going to do with it?"

"The private company that we own will license it to the Spain Green Building Council. They will be required to hire our firm to do the building inspections," he said with a smug look. "We've run the numbers and believe this will be a lucrative business for all of us. Our government will pay a lot of money for this system."

"There's no way I'd be part of a boondoggle like that," I shot back. "It's against our principles and it's unethical. Maybe this is how you do business in Spain, but in the U.S. we are careful about conflicts of interest. The council model requires that it be owned by a nonprofit in which all programs are open and consensus based. No one group can influence our standards or profit from our products." My words sounded pompous, but I meant them.

"You shouldn't dismiss our generous offer so quickly," the lawyer said sourly, his words mingling with smoke as he exhaled. "If you remain such a purist, you'll never make any money." He pointed his cigarette at me to emphasize his point.

"You've wasted your time. And you'll be receiving a bill from me for mine." I stuffed my papers into my briefcase.

"Aurelio?" the fish man asked. Aurelio's head popped out of his hands.

"I agree with David," he replied. "You guys are no longer part of the council." We left together with no goodbyes. When I glanced back, the three ousted members of the council sat shaking their heads and talking in rapid Spanish.

CHAPTER 15

Austin 2002

TWO YEARS HAD NOW PASSED. I'd gone on three speaking trips to Australia and helped launch the Green Building Council of Australia. Another GBC in Canada was in process. I had plenty of consulting projects, including the California Integrated Waste Management Board and Alameda County Waste Management projects, Williams Sonoma, Genentech, and Stanford University—their first campus green building, at Jasper Ridge Biological Preserve.

It was a decade since that cold night on the floor of Jeffrey's Marina apartment. I was now one of the longest-tenure tenants in my three-story walk-up. I'd never imagined I would be there an entire decade, and still single. I was now forty-two. My eldest brother, Rick, had gotten married five years earlier, and he and his wife now had a beautiful adopted boy, Gabriel. Glenn had been married seventeen years; we'd just celebrated his son Matt's Bar Mitzvah, and his daughter Leah was twelve. I found myself wondering if Matt would beat me to the altar.

In November 2002 I traveled to Austin, Texas, for the USGBC's First Annual International Conference (now called GreenBuild). As I walked from my hotel along Sixth Street toward downtown, I was amazed at the number of bars and clubs. It was 6:30 and the streets were fairly empty, though they would soon be filled with revelers: The University of Texas football team had won earlier that day. It was a party town, for sure.

I turned off on Red River Street, looking for a restaurant I was meeting some colleagues at. Above me, my eyes fell on a huge banner strung from lamppost to lamppost, at least fifty feet long and ten feet high. I figured it was announcing some local event, but the green-and-white symbol in the upper left looked familiar. I stopped in my tracks, a dazed joy spreading through my body. It was the council's round oak leaf logo, and the sign was announcing our conference in the Austin convention center. I trotted to the next main street and saw another banner swaying in the Texas sunshine. My heart beat rapidly. I got out my digital camera and shot a dozen photos. At one point, I stopped a passerby and asked him to take one of me in front of the sign. "I founded that group," I told him. He glanced at my jeans, at the banner, then shrugged and snapped the photo.

The next day, standing at the head of a large conference table, I welcomed twenty representatives from eight countries to a two-day WorldGBC meeting I'd organized to precede the USGBC conference. This time, I vowed I'd let the others lead the meeting, not drive the agenda myself as I'd done three years earlier. Instead I would be the courteous host and make sure my guests enjoyed themselves.

Kath Williams had helped me arrange for use of the Lady Bird Johnson Wildflower Center. It was the perfect spot: The flowing and colorful wildflower exhibition gardens were spectacular, and the scattered brick and concrete passive solar buildings were water and energy efficient, and included rainwater captured in a self-contained cistern. The room we were meeting in was lit by daylight, and the air smelled fresh and clean.

All that day, as founders of councils in Australia, Japan, Spain, the United States, Canada, Brazil, Mexico, and India (Korea had sent a briefing but was unable to attend) described their progress, I listened like a proud parent. The councils were at all phases of development, ranging from the USGBC, growing stronger by the day after almost a decade, to Brazil and Mexico, which had come to the meeting with the intention of learning the basics of a green building council.

I'd invited Nils Larsson, head of iiSBE (International Initiative for Sustainable Built Environment) in Ottawa, Canada. He and I had met earlier in the year in San Francisco to talk about how our organizations could work together. Now that Canada was forming its own green building council and was negotiating with USGBC to license LEED, we had even more in common. During the first day of the meeting, he informed us about his organization's technical activities, and then we proceeded to hammer out a memorandum of understanding between our two groups.

At each break, I walked around, listening to the conversations. Despite the many organizational and cultural differences, the participants had a remarkable rapport. Over the two days we met, I marveled at the strength of the bonds being created. These people shared passion, a pioneering spirit, and a determination to bring green buildings to their countries, despite the expense or hardship of the struggle.

That first evening, USGBC (the lead sponsor of the two-day WorldGBC meeting) hosted a banquet dinner for the international coalition, with welcoming remarks given by USGBC president and CEO, Christine Ervin. She enthusiastically supported our assembly and pledged the USGBC's full commitment. After several years of a wait-and-see attitude, our council had finally embraced the concept of the WorldGBC, agreeing to assume a leadership role and contribute seed money of $25,000. The WorldGBC (a "United Nations" of country GBCs), they realized, was a powerful way to share both information and green building tools. The USGBC already had an international base, and many of its members were glad to see our vision spread.

On the second day I woke up early, worrying. How could we get everyone to agree on our common organizational principles and structure? Our failure to accomplish this at the San Francisco meeting three years before was heavy on my mind. Despite my resolution to let things take their course, I had to do something, so I fired up my laptop and, gulping coffee, proceeded to list the dozen key organizational priorities as PowerPoint headers. They included mission, main programs, organizational structure, location, funding, founding board, officers, and strategic partners. This time though, I left the text blank. I'd let the group fill that in.

I had asked Maria Atkinson, executive director of the Green Building Council of Australia, and Nigel Howard, a vice president of the USGBC, to help me lead that day's discussion. (Nigel had moved from England to the United States to direct the LEED rating system program and its rapidly expanding staff in our D.C. office.) To keep myself from assuming control, I walked around the room with my camera, taking pictures. I also took numerous bathroom breaks and sat on my hands a lot in the back of the room, chatting with Rick Fedrizzi. At one point, Nigel said that we'd have to let each country organically develop its own version of a green building council, one that fit its culture. I wanted to interrupt and talk about common guidelines for all, but somehow managed to keep quiet. It wasn't my meeting; it was theirs. If there's one thing I had learned during my early years at the USGBC, it's that you can't bully people into moving faster than their natural pace—and you can't do everything yourself.

To my amazed delight, by the end of the day we'd progressed through almost all the topics I'd written down on my laptop that morning. People jumped into the discussion with enthusiasm, ideas came fast, and agreement followed quickly. "Raise your hand if you're in favor of the formation of the World Green Building Council," Maria said. I looked around the room. There was Raghu, the council founder from India—his firm, the Confederation of Indian Industry, represented over 4,800 companies with offices all over the world; Roberto, a leading architect from Brazil; Ishiguro and the ever-present Shisano; Rick Fedrizzi, sitting solidly at the end of the table; and a dozen more colleagues who today had joined together with passion to achieve a common goal. I couldn't breathe until I saw all hands raised high in the air. It was a beautiful sight.

All countries with councils would sit on the board. "And now," said Maria, "our officers." The slide projected on the screen listed several titles, starting with the chair. I stirred uneasily, desperately wanting to remain on the sidelines on this one.

It was no use. "You have no idea what David can do," Rick Fedrizzi said to the group. They looked at me with huge smiles.

"Everyone in favor of David as our chairman, raise your hand," Maria said. Everyone's hand shot into the air—except mine. When they started to clap, I shook my head. "What's wrong?" Maria asked.

"I can't do it." The room went silent; it was as if a cloud had passed beneath the sun. I felt a flush rising on my cheekbones. Their stillness brought the taste of iron into my mouth.

"We'll help you," Che said.

"Yes," Rick chimed in. "We'll do the work."

I felt a strong pull, like a riptide pulling me out to sea. I filled my lungs with oxygen—and said goodbye to my dream of freedom. "Okay," I said. Everybody cheered, and I tried to smile. But instead of joy, I felt a heaviness in my chest.

Two days later we had our first press briefing. I again took a seat in the back while a half dozen reporters in swivel chairs sat reading our newly drafted press release. "Get up there," Rick urged. I didn't know I was supposed to lead the briefing. The heat of the inefficient fluorescent lights beat on my head. On autopilot, I talked about the organization, then turned to my other comrades, letting each country's founder tell their own GBC story. When we'd finished talking, hands shot up.

"What is your political position?" one reported asked me. I froze. We didn't have one.

"We're not a political organization," I replied. I thought of all the wasted energy and time at the failed Earth Summit in Johannesburg that past August, as competing organizations and governments debated whether global warming existed and, if so, what the economic ramifications would be. "While others are debating and stalling, we're designing and building structures that lessen our global footprint. Green buildings can contribute up to a 40 percent reduction in a country's Kyoto Protocol commitment." As some of the other founders jumped in to expand on what I'd said, chills spread through my body. I was no longer alone!

The next morning I went for a run along the river. It reminded me of the Potomac: windy, with rowers streaking by on the water's surface. I waved to several USGBC acquaintances out walking. After a shower, I dressed and strolled over to the convention center. Inside I found myself greeting people on every hand: old friends, acquaintances, newcomers. It took me thirty minutes to make my way to the registration booth to pick up my name tag and meal tickets for the USGBC conference.

The first day was for members only. The council now had over 2,500 organizational members (within another year membership would stand at 3,500), and while we expected the turnout to be high, we were amazed to sell out the conference with 4,100 people in attendance, a number that exceeded our projections by a couple thousand. The trade expo, with two hundred booths, had also sold out. It was the largest green building event ever! Already, we were projecting 5,000 attendees and 350 booths at next year's event in Pittsburgh. I noticed the founders of the WorldGBC roaming the halls as a group. It reminded me of the early days of the USGBC, when we "greenies" would clump together at AIA's enormous national conventions.

The morning was given over to the council staff and committee heads briefing the members on our LEED program, with images projected on an enormous screen that hung from the ceiling. (The auditorium was so huge that, from the rear and even with my glasses on, I could barely make out the tiny figures onstage.)

They announced the rollout of LEED-NC version 2.1, a rating system for new construction and major renovations that would simplify the certification documentation paperwork. Loud applause welcomed the change. The speakers briefed us on the pilot programs for LEED-EB (Existing Building Operations) and LEED-CI (Commercial Interior Projects), and introduced us to new rating systems being developed for LEED-R (Retail) and LEED-CS (Core and Shell), as well as new initiatives just starting for LEED Homes and LEED Community.

The current LEED statistics were phenomenal: 600 LEED projects (up to 1,000 in September 2003), totaling over 80 million square feet of space (Nigel estimated this to account for about 4 percent of new construction in the United States, 130 million square feet by September 2003), in nine countries and forty-nine states. We now had thousands of LEED Accredited Professionals (4,700 by September 2003). LEED had been adopted as the official building performance standard in dozens of cities and at a dozen federal agencies. Interest in LEED was picking up in the private sector as well, as evidenced by the registration of dozens of projects on our Web site—though for every project that had paid us a registration fee, I guessed that five or more were using LEED as a free design tool. I knew that trend was a mixed blessing. On one hand, we knew that LEED's influence in the marketplace was even larger than we measured; on the other hand, these projects weren't taking advantage of the benefits from third-party certification, which would, in turn, propel the market ahead. The head of LEED-Retail was Ben Packard, the environmental affairs director at Starbucks whom I'd done some consulting for. He had formed a strong committee of retailers that included Home Depot, Williams Sonoma, Timberland, and L. L. Bean.

The council now had eighteen chapters; in addition, about two dozen provisional chapters were being organized, sometimes bursting beyond geopolitical boundaries—such as the Cascadia chapter, which encompassed Portland, Seattle, and Vancouver, B.C. After the members' lunch, representatives from each chapter displayed their official banner. I ran over to help hold the sign for the Northern California chapter. We already had a mailing list of about five hundred participants.

Then I ventured onto that enormous stage to introduce the world green building councils as our reach went global. My new friends stood on their chairs and cheered loudly.

I took my seat, and Bob Berkebile came to the podium. We'd met in 1991 at AIA, after he'd founded its Committee on the Environment. He was there during that tense first meeting in 1993 with the AIA leadership in D.C., and we had worked together on the Montana State University project. He had recently joined the board of USGBC.

"We'd like to present leadership awards to our founders, chairman, and officers," he announced. I was the first to be called up. Bob introduced me by saying, "I met this young man who had a vision of greening the U.S. building industry. I didn't know what to make of him and his promise, but he had a lot of passion and was good at recruiting us." After me came Mike (he'd missed the conference due to work back in D.C. with his company, the Sustainable Products Corporation. Several years ago Mike had left his law firm and founded his own leading-edge green products consulting and training company). Next was Rick Fedrizzi, then Steven Winter, Kath Williams, and Keith Winn, with Herman Miller furniture. Keith had become his company's lead council representative several years earlier, and was now our treasurer. I felt extremely honored as Bob presented me with a beautiful glass sculpture that spelled out USGBC, our round logo on its base and a green glass replicate of our logo's oak leaf set off to the right. "For extraordinary and sustained service" was engraved on mine, along with my name and the title "Founder."

A hundred educational sessions in a dozen tracks filled the next two days. It was the world's most extensive green building university. We'd had trouble selecting all the sessions, there were so many submissions—over six hundred. I facilitated two of the sessions. The rest of the time I mingled, saying hello to hundreds of friends, my head swimming with names and affiliations.

My girlfriend, Sara Szal, arrived toward the end of the conference. We'd met through Match.com, an Internet dating service with over a million members. Although we'd spoken on the phone as early as April 2002, for various reasons we didn't actually meet until August.

When I accessed her Internet dating profile, I learned that Sara was a gynecologist at Kaiser, that she loved nature, yoga, and art and was looking for a partner to explore the deeper meaning of life with. She also wanted someone to help her raise her two-and-a-half-year-old daughter, Gemma, a bright-eyed blonde sprite with a mischievous grin. I wasn't sure I was ready for that, but I finally decided to take the chance and at least meet Sara. After all, what did I have to lose?

We arranged to get together for coffee in the Rockridge neighborhood of Oakland where she and Gemma lived. I was early, so I sat down on the curb in front of the restaurant and waited nervously. Would I feel a spark? Would we have anything in common, or would the date be a dud—my usual experience with blind dating.

"Hey," I heard from above. I looked up at a woman with dark flowing hair and big gleaming blue-green eyes. I scrambled to my feet.

We talked for three hours. Coffee became brunch, after which we walked over to her small 1910 cottage. She'd planted a garden, and clothes were drying on the line. A mountain bike was parked out front. Gemma's toys, dolls, and artwork were scattered through the house, as were books and magazines. I saw a pile of *New Yorkers* and a shelf of books on Judaism. Several were by Abraham Heschel. Sara had a hair appointment, so I walked her there. "This has been wonderful," I said. I reached out for a hug, and instead kissed her on the lips. Electricity crackled through my synapses. "Wow!" I gasped. She pulled me closer.

I didn't want our first date to end — and it hasn't. I was thrilled that she wanted to join me at the Austin conference: It felt like an important personal milestone, right up there with the professional milestone that this gathering represented for me. And mixing the two together put me on top of the world.

The last night of the Austin conference, I would be giving out green leadership awards, so I wore my sage textured suit, gold tie, and a dark-green textured shirt I'd bought in Melbourne earlier that year. My USGBC member pin shone from the lapel. Sara was beautiful in a long black dress, white pearls, and her "up-do" hair. It was our coming out: She'd never attended a council event, and I'd never brought a date before. We strolled hand in hand from the hotel to the ballroom at the convention center.

Inside, we were swamped: Everyone wanted to meet Sara. She handled herself as if this was an everyday occurrence. Finally, we took our seats at the head table. There was a roar of voices, like waves on the shore, as people at the two hundred or so tables talked and laughed.

My mouth was dry and I was fiddling with the silverware, nervous and revved up, as always, before giving a speech. I sipped my wine to calm my nerves. Sara, who was chatting away with Rick

Fedrizzi, reached over and squeezed my hand. They were meeting for the first time. At one point I looked over and he mouthed the words, "I love her. She's wonderful." Later he told me Sara was exactly the type of woman he always knew I'd end up with: attractive, smart, passionate, committed to making the world a better place, and her own person.

"Now I'd like to call up our founder, David Gottfried," the M.C., John Bevilaqua, announced. I climbed up the stairs to the stage. Once there, for a minute all I could see was the bright lights. When my eyes adjusted, I had the shock of seeing my face projected on the huge hanging video screen. I could even see the bags under my eyes.

Then my autopilot feature took over as I grabbed both sides of the lectern and looked out at our congregation of "greenies." I felt like the rabbi my mother had always wanted me to be. I began my sermon. "A decade ago, green building was considered the arcane interest of a few environmental organizations and architects. Today, we have become our own industry," I said. The room was silent. I felt Sara's presence and glanced over at our table. She was gazing at me, smiling, her eyes shining. I gave her a little hand wave to the side of the podium. She waved back, and my heart sang.

After my remarks, I introduced the first annual green building leadership awards. The USGBC Lifetime Leadership Award went to our chair of the LEED rating system, Rob Watson. LEED had enabled the U.S. building industry to begin its transformation from conventional to green, and it was the tool that put the council on the global map. Rob and I hugged as I handed him his award. He felt like a brother. When he spoke to those assembled, he broke out in tears. I shared his joy.

Pliny Fisk, an Austinite, won our Green Public Service Award for nongovernmental organizations for his thirty years of pioneering work in green building. Our Green Public Service Government Award (accepted in absentia) went to New York governor George Pataki for his leadership in passing the nation's first green building tax credit. Ray Anderson won the Green Business Award for greening Interface company-wide and for the company's environmental carpet offerings.

After the event, Sara and I walked in the moonlight with Rick back to the hotel. "Do you know what you've done?" Rick asked. I looked at him.

"You've changed the world," he said. Sara squeezed my hand. "You've done what people only dream of doing in a lifetime."

My heart rose in my throat. "I couldn't have done it without you," I managed to get out.

The founders of the WorldGBC were sitting together in the lobby of the hotel. When they asked us to join them for a drink, Sara nudged me. I got the message. I said my goodbyes and pushed the elevator button to deliver us into our future.

CHAPTER 16

Greening My Life

We must be the change we wish to see.
—Gandhi

IN SEPTEMBER 2003 I rented a jeep and drove to my favorite camping site on the Pit River. I sat on a large boulder, rigging my fishing rod and breathing in the scent of the pine trees. I had a good feeling about the day—the water was cool, the sky clear. I was fishing in a part of the river that others avoid because of slick round boulders that make wading difficult and falling likely. It was my kind of river.

Trying to gauge the correct distance, I made several false casts before hitting the pool. My fly landed lightly and was tugged downstream by the current. I watched the artificial bug bobbing in the white water and thought back to my final, most urgent idea: the greening of my life.

The process started in Spain in 2000. After that horrible SpainGBC meeting in Madrid, I took the high-speed train to Seville. Over Christmas I sat in a cold, dark hotel room for several days, unable to shake an attack of flu—the fourth that year. It was pouring rain, making it unpleasant to venture through the winding streets of the old city. In the half light of that shadowy room,

I encountered a stranger in the mirror, with bags under his eyes, blown-out facial features, and an appearance of general exhaustion. My immune system was trashed from years of travel and stress. I was still single and very much alone. My relationships never progressed past a few months, when the real work commenced and I said, "Here's your key back."

Sitting in that room, I realized that the lessons of conservation, preservation, and restoration in green building had not made their way into my own life. I was good at recycling paper and plastic and using minimal energy, but I failed to recycle and preserve myself when depleted or hurting. My way was to charge forward full speed ahead. Even when biking with a sore back, I went for the steep hills rather than the level paths. I later learned that all of my energy was what the Chinese call *yang:* masculine, hard driving, depleting. Missing from my life was the more feminine side, *yin:* nurturing, loving, and enhancing.

I always had to be the best, the brightest, the fastest, the strongest. This meant getting up in the morning before work, when it was still dark and cold, and running for an hour—often seven days a week. Once I tracked my routine for a year and was proud that I'd gone running three hundred days. I didn't stop even when sick.

All through meetings my mind would race as I calculated how I could distinguish myself—get my A. I learned to speak in a commanding manner, to take control and dazzle everyone with my brilliance. Keeping silent when I had a point to make was impossible. I wanted all in the room and certainly the top executives to be wowed by my ideas and my energy. It was easy to identify the other overachievers. They were similarly outspoken and controlling, sitting poised on the edge of their seats to get a word in. If others were not paying attention or were slow to comprehend, I became frustrated. On occasions when I was the lead facilitator, in my early years, I was not open enough to let others fully contribute. My arrogance made me think one had to go to a top university or be rich in order to have anything valuable to say.

Sadly, however, even when I got what I wanted—the recognition, the accolades, the contract, the money—my feeling of elation was only momentary. Within a day or two, and sometimes within only a few hours, I was hungry again for the next challenge.

This drive allowed me to achieve more than other people, but at a cost. The competitive juices burned me up inside. Caffeine helped prop me up, so I drank it constantly. It hurt my stomach, but I failed to notice this side effect for twenty years. For a long time, the signs of fractures were evident: a weak stomach, back constantly in spasm, poor sleep, and a hot temper.

I not only yielded to the pressure of my own competitive, driving nature, but also expected others to do the same. I was a tough boss. I held my employees, as well as my family, friends, and associates, to ridiculously high standards. One of my project managers, Huston, was an exemplary employee and friend, yet I pushed him so hard he quit. He didn't like chasing clients for past-due payments on work we'd performed, and instead of relenting and doing it myself, I tried to force him to do it. I was not capable of accepting no for an answer, nor could I admit to the notion of gray zones: Everything was either black or white. People had to behave as I expected them to, or I would become frustrated.

To comfort myself, I would lock the door and curl up on the couch with videos; it never occurred to me to seek out other people or get help.

After Spain, however, all that changed. I resolved to make *myself* into a greening project. As with my building work, I assembled a "green team": I found a physician who stresses preventive health care, a chiropractor, a life coach, and an acupuncturist. I started back at the gym. To boost my immune system, the doctor put me on a cleansing diet: no sugar, alcohol, caffeine, or lactose products for three months. I reestablished regular calls with a psychiatrist I'd seen during those turbulent days when Karen was tormenting me in D.C. "Stop seeking perfection in all you do," he now advised me. "We don't want to be talking about the same issues in *another* ten years, do we?"

I found a local haven, a place called Inverness. It's adjacent to the Point Reyes National Seashore, an hour northwest of San Francisco. I rented a small yurt perched atop a mountain ridge, overlooking a valley of lush greenness. The hot tub helped soak away the layers of stress, and I learned to take it easy and be kind to myself. How great it felt to luxuriate in a cabin without a phone or Internet access, removed from all urban noise and pressure! Daily hikes, naps, and a healthy diet were part of the new routine. I began dabbling with yoga and meditation. Even my stride slowed, and my hikes became strolls with neither destination nor time goal. "I'm working at becoming an underachiever," I said to a friend. "I'm trying to be less competitive. Naps have replaced another cup of coffee. I try to listen."

I told my life coach, Dorothy, I wanted to write a book about my journey. "If you want to be a writer, make time for it," she replied. "Show me what you're going to quit. It has to become part of your work life, not something you just do on the side. If you're serious, you need to show commitment to change." In mid-2001, vowing to dedicate 50 percent of my day to writing, I pulled back from full-time consulting.

My mother has been battling breast cancer. In mid-2002 she had a mastectomy, followed by months of chemotherapy. Toward the end of her treatment they found cancer in her other breast.

Her strength amazes me. "I'm not worried about the procedure. I'm a good patient," she remarked with each surgery. Within a few days after her surgeries she'd be back playing cards with her friends and going to plays and movies with my dad. Her illness brought us closer. During our daily calls we shared intimate details of our lives, and learned to truly support each other. By observing her "quiet" strength, I realized that she too had been a steady force and foundation to my life. While my dad taught me business skills, Mom showed me how to love.

My father is short of breath due to his partial lung and being out of shape. His hobby—making model trains and buildings for a miniature city he designed, with hundreds of glued-together and painted parts—doesn't help. "We're taking turns," Mom said one day after visiting Dad in the hospital, where he was being tested for symptoms of a heart attack. "When he was off taking his tests, I climbed into his hospital bed and had the best rest. It was delicious."

Since the surgeries my parents say "I love you" at the end of each phone call. We now speak almost daily. Sometimes they irritate me, but I can't stop calling. Our love is part of my oxygen intake. It's the same with my two brothers. When someone you love gets cancer, the emotional weight of that diagnosis fills your consciousness. A message is delivered: Slow down and taste life's offerings. I hear it each day.

I needed to cast my dad as a one-dimensional businessman so I would have a frame to cast my own life against. He had to be the dark, so I could be the light. Now I realize I am like my dad—that is, I hope I am like him. My ethics come from him. He's the one who taught me to be accountable. When you design a building that doesn't pollute, you are accountable.

I was discouraged by my first three attempts at writing this book. For eighteen months I wrote text that was impersonal and stiff. My good friend and teacher, Mischa, would write in the margin, "Excellent reporting; but where are you?" That was a good question. I was trying to get my A, as opposed to being myself. It was hard to let my heart pour out, when I was so removed and unavailable.

Of course, I can't stop being myself, so perhaps it isn't surprising that even this most personal of quests resulted in another invention. One day at the Inverness yurt I sat down with my laptop on a deck overlooking the valley below. As I watched hawks ride the wind above me, I felt a surge of excitement—and the birth of an idea. From my work in green building, I had helped create a LEED system to guide desired change in how we designed our buildings, one that provided both a destination and an assessment tool. What if I did the same with my personal greening work?

The Life Balance Sheet (LBS) was the result—or, as I later called it, LEED Life. It's s a 100-point rating system to gauge my life's overall sustainability. Like LEED, it has four award levels: Certified, 60–69; Silver, 70–79; Gold, 80–89; and Platinum, 90–100.

I identified ten categories of life importance (10 points each): health, mental and emotional development, work, finances, social life, cultural development, fun, compassion and giving, eco-sustainability, and personal contentment. My initial score was 58 points: I wasn't even living a *Certified* sustainable life. After two years of diligent effort, my score improved by 45 percent, to 84. Now I was living a *Gold* life!

How did I improve? Well, it required a high level of awareness and commitment as I identified and then focused on all the things that truly matter in life, and worked to make changes that I knew were right for me.

The first category is health, whose subcategories are stress, fitness level, exercise, diet, sleep, physical ailments, anger management, and a comfortable home. My "green team" helped me heal my ailments (stomach, back, anger). Working at a less hectic pace, following the Atkins diet, and maintaining a regular exercise routine led to better sleep and less stress. I rearranged my apartment to separate my work area from my personal space, and bought a fountain to remind me to slow down and relax.

The next category is mental and emotional development. It includes reading and continual learning, self-exploration, ongoing challenges, opportunities to be creative, and emotional growth. Writing this book pushed up my score in all of these areas. My first two years of writing were therapeutic, even though I didn't produce any finished text. I first needed to cleanse myself by pouring out built-up anger, disappointment, and pain. This process allowed me to shed false layers and identify and then dispel internal demons that hold me back from growth and contentment. My work with Dorothy and my shrink, and my relationship with Sara also boosted my emotional maturity.

The next category is work: feeling productive and challenged as you earn your living, while being able to exercise individual control and flexibility; having high-caliber coworkers, sufficient pay, and financial equity or leverage potential; and working in a nontoxic setting, with eco-friendly services and products. I've enjoyed my work as a green consultant, public speaker, and now writer. The nonprofit work with helping found green building councils gave me added purpose and fulfillment, as well as a positive challenge. In June 2003, I set up a small, soulful (and green) office on the twelfth floor of a historic building in Berkeley, with a view of the bay and downtown San Francisco. It sits on top of a BART metro stop, and has ample daylighting and cross ventilation. My work involves constant collaboration with others—mostly those committed to green. The money as a consultant is good, though it lacks the equity-building leverage I had as a real estate developer; one item on my list, therefore, is to explore more green leverage equity opportunities. As my own boss, I work long hours, but I have lots of control and flexibility.

The next category is financial; if you're broke and can't do what you want or support your family, that's not a green life. I've always lived within my means and usually made a good income, except some of those years when we were creating the USGBC. My consulting work has slowed down due to my 50 percent writing commitment—but if you're reading this, that has been a good investment. I'm starting to plan for my future and retirement.

Social life is next. Much of life is about love: of friends, family, and a partner. I've always been close to my immediate family, and now, as we all grow older, we've become even closer. Sara and Gemma have been the greatest addition to my life. After ten years living in my Marina bachelor apartment, I eagerly moved into their small Rockridge cottage. Sara and I were married at our own green wedding in October 2003, and I became a stepfather. These days I'm awakened by the sound of Gemma's little footsteps and the words "Mommy, *juicey.*" In another year or two, we plan to increase the chorus at home. I've learned to open up and rely more on a few close friends, who in turn have become part of my extended family.

Cultural development is part of overall balance: reading, music and theater, travel, and spiritual development. My score has remained flat in this area over the past few years as I've limited foreign travel but increased reading, music, and spiritual development. "What about religion and faith?" a student asked me not too long ago during a lecture I gave on the Life Balance Sheet. "I'm a

Christian and my faith is very important to me," she said. Even though I am Jewish, I have always regarded nature as my "religion": I feel the most spiritual when I am in the natural world. It is my temple, and I hear God's words in the sound of the wind in the trees and the flow of water. Nature teaches me to live sustainably, taking only what I need. However, I have subsequently amended the system to include spiritual development. I would like to further explore my Judaism and its connection to green.

The fun category includes sports and games, outdoor recreation, vacations, socializing, and hobbies. I've always loved sports. I keep up my fly-fishing, hiking, and camping; and play an occasional round of golf. Twice a week I bike Gemma to breakfast and then to preschool, and weekends often find the three of us hiking in Tilden Park. Dancing with Gemma at 6:30 in the morning is also irresistible. Sara loves to vacation, and we've kept an active travel pace to localities around California and the big island of Hawaii for the honeymoon. We also socialize regularly with friends and my five sets of cousins in the Bay Area.

The next LBS category is compassion and giving. During my D.C. years of real estate and then as I concentrated on greening the building industry, my work rarely focused on social causes. Even over the past decade, although I worked in green, I failed to make a direct connection between my work and helping people. They are, however, most definitely connected. Once I came to realize this, I increased my mentoring and began giving more local university lectures. Sara, Gemma, and I will soon be moving to a new, "green" house, and once we get settled I plan to spend more time focusing on community—investing myself locally, where we live. I've worked hard to be more open and available, though I still catch myself becoming self-absorbed. Unfortunately, it is likely to be a life struggle.

The next category relates closest to my work over the past decade: eco-sustainability. It also has the most subcategories: overall footprint on Earth (car gas mileage, amount of commuting by means other than automobile, level of material consumption, the "eco-nature" of work, home size and energy and water efficiency, level of recycling and reuse); contribution to environmental organizations; awareness of the environmental state of the world and dedication to making life better for others. As you might expect, I did all right in this category.

The last category is the most important: contentment. The subcategories include inner peace, fulfillment and achievement, making a difference, living life according to your personal values, self-knowledge, and growth and risk taking. I've improved in this category, but of course I'd like to score higher. However, achieving contentment is our life's work.

The fly floats lazily across the pool in front of me. As it passes, I see a reflection in the water. The face looks familiar, but different. I recognize the dark hair and the general features. However, the eyes are changed. They are at once radiant and full of life, yet peaceful.

I continue casting. My movements are fluid, marked by a steady and natural rhythm. I hit the middle of a small pool. My fly finds the bubble line and moves downstream.

The sudden rise of a large rainbow trout jolts me and I raise my rod and set the hook. The fish sprints downriver as my fly line rips out of the spool. I pull in line as fast as possible. The fish feels the increased pressure and leaps into the air with all its wild strength. I pull in more line and raise my rod tip high. The rainbow darts deep into fast-moving water. As I fight to maintain control, the fly pops out of its mouth. The fish dives deep to freedom, blending in with its surroundings.

My heart is beating rapidly. I take several deep breaths and think about the beauty of the fish: its wildness, amazing spirit and courage, the vibrancy of its colors, and the depth of its survival instinct.

I realize that I have tapped into the same spirit—that of nature and wildness. My soul has found its way home. Like the trout, I have broken free!

About the Author

DAVID GOTTFRIED is the president of
WorldBuild Technologies Inc., based in
Berkeley, California. Since the firm's founding in 1994, WorldBuild
has served as the sustainable consultant for many leading projects,
including several award winners. Clients include Starbucks,
DreamWorks SKG, Stanford University, Williams-Sonoma, Genentech, the State of California and San Diego Gas & Electric.

David founded the U.S. Green Building Council. The USGBC
is the leading green building organization in the United States,
with approximately 3,500 organizational members from all sectors of the building industry. He also created the World Green
Building Council, with councils being developed in eight countries. David is the founding chairman of ASTM's Green Building
Committee and the managing editor of the U.S. DOE- and EPA-
funded *Sustainable Building Technical Manual*.